D0403193

Additional praise for
Predictive Business Analytics:
Forward-Looking Capabilities to Improve Business Performance

"In the words of Harvard Professor MENG Xiao-Li (quoted by Thomas Davenport), 'you don't need to become a winemaker to become a wine connoisseur.' This book constitutes an excellent introduction to anyone wishing to grow into a data connoisseur. Skipping all the technical aspects of predictive analytics, it focusses on how to better appreciate quantitative analysis, allowing readers to become more sophisticated consumers of data. A first-class and extremely enlightening read about fact-based decision making."

—Dr. Olivier Maugain, CEO, AsiaAnalytics (formerly SPSS China)

"The authors make a compelling case: to win in tomorrow's marketplace, a company must know—not just guess at—the ways in which non-financial factors will impact financial results. But many managers will fail to adjust to this new decision-making paradigm. Reading this book is your first step in avoiding that fate. The authors use an engaging writing style and tons of practical examples to provide a clear picture of the competencies and skills sets you need to succeed."

—Mary Driscoll, Senior Research Fellow, APQC

"Simply put, Larry and Gary have nailed the 'why' and the 'how' of Predictive Business Analytics in this publication. To be an economically viable company in today's transparent, global and competitive world, business leaders must champion the predictive analytics journey and embed this powerful management practice as an operational core competency. The companies that thrive integrate predictive business analytics into their DNA to out-smart their competitors in strategic and tactical decision making that yields sustainable success."

—Chris D. Fraga, Chief Strategy Officer and President,
Acorn International

Wiley & SAS Business Series

The Wiley & SAS Business Series presents books that help senior-level managers with their critical management decisions.

Titles in the Wiley and SAS Business Series include:

Activity-Based Management for Financial Institutions: Driving Bottom-Line Results by Brent Bahnub

Big Data Analytics: Turning Big Data into Big Money by Frank Ohlhorst

Branded! How Retailers Engage Consumers with Social Media and Mobility by Bernie Brennan and Lori Schafer

Bricks Matter: The Role of Supply Chains in Building Market-Driven Differentiation by Lora M. Cecere and Charles W. Chase

Business Analytics for Customer Intelligence by Gert Laursen

Business Analytics for Managers: Taking Business Intelligence beyond Reporting by Gert Laursen and Jesper Thorlund

The Business Forecasting Deal: Exposing Bad Practices and Providing Practical Solutions by Michael Gilliland

Business Intelligence Applied: Implementing an Effective Information and Communications Technology Infrastructure by Michael S. Gendron

Business Intelligence Success Factors: Tools for Aligning Your Business in the Global Economy by Olivia Parr Rud

CIO Best Practices: Enabling Strategic Value with Information Technology, Second Edition by Joe Stenzel

Connecting Organizational Silos: Taking Knowledge Flow Management to the Next Level with Social Media by Frank Leistner

Credit Risk Assessment: The New Lending System for Borrowers, Lenders, and Investors by Clark Abrahams and Mingyuan Zhang

Credit Risk Scorecards: Developing and Implementing Intelligent Credit Scoring by Naeem Siddiqi

The Data Asset: How Smart Companies Govern Their Data for Business Success by Tony Fisher

Delivering Business Analytics: Practical Guidelines for Best Practice by Evan Stubbs

Demand-Driven Forecasting: A Structured Approach to Forecasting, Second Edition by Charles Chase

Demand-Driven Inventory Optimization and Replenishment: Creating a More Efficient Supply Chain by Robert A. Davis

The Executive's Guide to Enterprise Social Media Strategy: How Social Networks Are Radically Transforming Your Business by David Thomas and Mike Barlow

Executive's Guide to Solvency II by David Buckham, Jason Wahl, and Stuart Rose

Fair Lending Compliance: Intelligence and Implications for Credit Risk Management by Clark R. Abrahams and Mingyuan Zhang

Foreign Currency Financial Reporting from Euros to Yen to Yuan: A Guide to Fundamental Concepts and Practical Applications by Robert Rowan

Health Analytics: Gaining the Insights to Transform Health Care by Jason Burke

Human Capital Analytics: How to Harness the Potential of Your Organization's Greatest Asset by Gene Pease, Boyce Byerly, and Jac Fitz-enz

Information Revolution: Using the Information Evolution Model to Grow Your Business by Jim Davis, Gloria J. Miller, and Allan Russell

Killer Analytics: Top 20 Metrics Missing from Your Balance Sheet by Mark G. Brown

Manufacturing Best Practices: Optimizing Productivity and Product Quality by Bobby Hull

Marketing Automation: Practical Steps to More Effective Direct Marketing by Jeff LeSueur

Mastering Organizational Knowledge Flow: How to Make Knowledge Sharing Work by Frank Leistner

The New Know: Innovation Powered by Analytics by Thornton May

Performance Management: Integrating Strategy Execution, Methodologies, Risk, and Analytics by Gary Cokins

Retail Analytics: The Secret Weapon by Emmett Cox

Social Network Analysis in Telecommunications by Carlos Andre Reis Pinheiro

Statistical Thinking: Improving Business Performance, Second Edition by Roger W. Hoerl and Ronald D. Snee

Taming the Big Data Tidal Wave: Finding Opportunities in Huge Data Streams with Advanced Analytics by Bill Franks

Too Big to Ignore: The Business Case for Big Data by Phil Simon

The Value of Business Analytics: Identifying the Path to Profitability by Evan Stubbs

Visual Six Sigma: Making Data Analysis Lean by Ian Cox, Marie A. Gaudard, Philip J. Ramsey, Mia L. Stephens, and Leo Wright

Win with Advanced Business Analytics: Creating Business Value from Your Data by Jean Paul Isson and Jesse Harriott

For more information on any of the above titles, please visit **www.wiley.com.**

Predictive Business Analytics

Forward-Looking Capabilities to
Improve Business Performance

Lawrence S. Maisel
Gary Cokins

Cover image: © iStockphoto.com/peepo
Cover design: Michael Rutkowski

Copyright © 2014 by Lawrence S. Maisel and Gary Cokins.

Published by John Wiley & Sons, Inc., Hoboken, New Jersey.
Published simultaneously in Canada.

No part of this publication may be reproduced, stored in a retrieval system,
or transmitted in any form or by any means, electronic, mechanical,
photocopying, recording, scanning, or otherwise, except as permitted under
Section 107 or 108 of the 1976 United States Copyright Act, without either the
prior written permission of the Publisher, or authorization through payment
of the appropriate per-copy fee to the Copyright Clearance Center, Inc., 222
Rosewood Drive, Danvers, MA 01923, (978) 750-8400, fax (978) 646-8600, or
on the Web at www.copyright.com. Requests to the Publisher for permission
should be addressed to the Permissions Department, John Wiley & Sons, Inc.,
111 River Street, Hoboken, NJ 07030, (201) 748-6011, fax (201) 748-6008, or
online at http://www.wiley.com/go/permissions.

Limit of Liability/Disclaimer of Warranty: While the publisher and author have
used their best efforts in preparing this book, they make no representations
or warranties with respect to the accuracy or completeness of the contents of
this book and specifically disclaim any implied warranties of merchantability
or fitness for a particular purpose. No warranty may be created or extended
by sales representatives or written sales materials. The advice and strategies
contained herein may not be suitable for your situation. You should consult
with a professional where appropriate. Neither the publisher nor author shall
be liable for any loss of profit or any other commercial damages, including but
not limited to special, incidental, consequential, or other damages.

For general information on our other products and services or for technical
support, please contact our Customer Care Department within the United
States at (800) 762-2974, outside the United States at (317) 572-3993 or fax
(317) 572-4002.

Wiley publishes in a variety of print and electronic formats and by print-on-
demand. Some material included with standard print versions of this book
may not be included in e-books or in print-on-demand. If this book refers to
media such as a CD or DVD that is not included in the version you purchased,
you may download this material at http://booksupport.wiley.com. For more
information about Wiley products, visit www.wiley.com.

ISBN 978-1-118-17556-9 (Hardcover)
ISBN 978-1-118-22711-4 (ePDF)
ISBN 978-1-118-24015-1 (ePub)

Printed in the United States of America

10 9 8 7 6 5 4 3 2 1

I would like to dedicate this book to my wife, Claudia, whose patience and intelligence have always been a source of inspiration. I also want to acknowledge my parents and brother, who provided gentle guidance, and my children, Nicole, Dana, and Jonathan, who always bring out the best in me.

Lawrence S. Maisel

I express my thanks in remembrance to Bob Bonsack, my true mentor at Deloitte and EDS, for educating and training me in business methods and bringing value to people. I also thank my wife, Pam Tower, for her endless patience when I am distracted with projects such as writing this book.

Gary Cokins

Contents

Preface

An organization's ability to learn, and translate that learning into action rapidly, is the ultimate competitive advantage.

—Jack Welch

"Apple's Steve Jobs was known to explicitly discount the value of surveys and focus groups for designing new products. How do you explain this apparent anti-empiricism? One explanation is that, much like a creative scientist, people like Jobs recognize when there is not enough data or the right kind of data to form a theory. They recognize that, for completely new lines of products that will change a user's experience or behavior, the only useful data is experiential data, not commentary and reactions from those who have never used the product.

This approach to decision making using empiricism and analytics might seem like a death knell for such vaunted business traits as intuition, gut feel, killer instinct, and so forth, right? Not so fast! Business decision making can be purely empirical and dispassionate, but decision makers are not. Sound decision making favors those who are creative, are intuitive, and can take a leap of faith.

The enterprise of the future, based on empiricism and analytical decision making, will indeed be considerably different from today's enterprise."[1] In the future, even more than today, businesses will be expected to possess the talent, tools, processes, and capabilities to enable their organizations to implement and utilize continuous analysis of past business performance and events to gain forward-looking insight to drive business decisions and actions.

Over the years, we have been working with companies like yours to gain deeper insights and understand the dynamics related to managing operations, controlling cost, increasing profit margins, and leveraging data-driven analytics. We've helped companies enhance employees' skills and competencies, and managers and staff to improve their organization's performance and the effectiveness of their decision making. Along with contributing author Eileen Morrissey, we have been at the forefront of important contributions to management practices, including activity-based costing and enterprise performance management, including balanced scorecards.

Now we have embarked on an additional path along this career journey by writing this book on *predictive business analytics* (PBA). Although in today's parlance the term *analytics* can be associated with any number of business methods and practices as well as software tools, we have sought to distinguish PBA from other related business practices such as enterprise performance management, driver-based forecasting, business intelligence, predictive analytics, and so on (see Part Four for a fuller discussion on those topics) because its effectiveness as a recognized business practice will be sustainable only if it demonstrates how it contributes to value and growth.

In fact, many recent surveys are quantifying just how valuable PBA has become as a contributor to the success of a business. In one survey, 90 percent of respondents attained a positive ROI from their most successful deployment of predictive analytics, and more than half from their *least* successful deployment.[2] In another survey, "Among respondents who have implemented predictive business analytics, 66% say it provides 'very high' or 'high' business value."[3] And alarmingly, in another survey, "respondents that have not yet adopted predictive technologies experienced a 2% decline in profit margins, and a 1% drop in their customer retention rate."[4]

In fact, case examples after case examples are demonstrating that for a company to use PBA effectively it must commit to a sustained and rigorous process in order to achieve meaningful results. This includes the ability to establish a team of individuals with complementary skills and competencies, a repeatable set of practices, functional data and tools, and (importantly) a management process to review its results and forge its decision making by leveraging these results and insights (see Part Three: Case Studies). Together, these are used to analyze continuously the right business and cost drivers and measures that have a strong cause-and-effect relationship to gain insight to better manage the business and to improve decision making.

A widely accepted best practice is to embed predictive business analytics models in operational systems for use in decision management. Key business decisions need to be made with their likely expectation of outcomes or results—from possibilities to probabilities. PBA is a backbone to enable more effective analysis and decision making that recognize how the future might play out. PBA should (1) reflect the needs of business users, (2) be the result of a consistent and trusted process, and (3) represent the appropriate time frame for the decisions being made. Users need meaningful data at the right time and in a form they can rely on. For PBA information to be meaningful, it should be tailored to the designated consumers of that information in a form and context that describe the outcomes, causes, and consequences of decisions and actions associated with alternative future drivers (amounts or quantities) and business conditions. Information should be presented in a manner that conveys the key messages and portrays the alternative actions in an unambiguous and straightforward manner, using formats that are graphic and intuitively understood.

For example, in traveling to a business meeting, the driver sees a series of data points on an automobile dashboard (e.g., gauges for speed, engine temperature, oil pressure). These may be complete, but unless they inform the user of the range of acceptable tolerances and the implications related to the situation (e.g., highway versus bumpy country road), they will usually not be sufficient for meaningful decision making and actions about safety and timely arrival. Building on this example, PBA can be expanded to provide alerts and suggested alternative decisions and actions that might be considered. Another example might be a health care organization analyzing its staffing needs; it will likely gather data about its (1) service area population (e.g., age, ethnicity, gender) and (2) present and future health care reimbursement contracts and conditions. These attributes (and others) will enable the organization to better select the range of options regarding its longer-term staffing levels, competencies and skills requirements, and specialties, as well as service-level capacities (e.g., number of beds) in each of these specialty areas.

The data from the analysis should be useful to the user or it will not be used. The tolerance of the ranges needs to be "fit for purpose." For example, predicting required production volumes by location for next week's operating plans and scheduling is different from predicting revenues six months forward.

In contrast, James Taylor, coauthor of *Smart (Enough) Systems*,[5] categorizes business intelligence in a more limited light and concludes that "insights delivered by standard business intelligence and reporting are not readily actionable; they must be translated to action by way of human judgment. Metrics, reports, dashboards, and other retrospective analyses are important components of enterprise business intelligence, but their execution is ad hoc in that it is not clear a priori what kind of actions or decisions will be recommended, if any."[6]

Many years ago, we learned that for a theory to be applied in business, it must be practical and implementable with a reasonable allocation of resources. It is no different with PBA, which is most impactful when it supports business decisions that can be acted upon (e.g., open a new market, hire additional sales personnel, invest in new products, close down a factory, and so on). As a result, PBA's true value is in its practical and implementable application, which will be discussed in the book.

The PBA theory likely has numerous originators and proponents. However, for us, our origination started more formally with a request from the Financial and Performance Management Task Force of the International Federation of Accountants (IFAC), chaired by Eileen Morrissey and directed by IFAC's Stathis Gould, to author an International Good Practice Guidance entitled "Predictive Business Analytics,"[7] published in October 2011. This was an 18-month process to determine guiding principles (see Chapter 3) and summarize important frameworks and practices for these principles with Morrissey, Gould, and their other task force members providing ongoing support and contributions to refine the guidance. In Chapters 4 and 5, we expand on these principles and approaches for deploying PBA.

What followed was the opportunity for us to coauthor a book that leverages these principles with real-world experiences and illustrates, through case studies and exhibits, materials that can be used as adaptable templates. We address how PBA integrates with several important business management and improvement methods and techniques in Part Four, and conclude in Part Five with chapters that anticipate trends and recognize organizational challenges.

Our intent is to:

- Build a growing body of knowledge on PBA.
- Clarify how PBA and other uses of analytics such as predictive analytics and business intelligence are related but differ in substance and application.
- Highlight success stories and relevant survey data that demonstrate how a company deploys PBA to realize its full potential and value.

However, our most important commitment is to motivate and challenge our readers to agree, disagree, and improve or refine the principles and practices we present. Each step in this process helps to further that body of knowledge to foster more competitive and stronger organizations. We hope that you find the discussions and case studies rewarding and that they enable you to participate in the furtherance of this game-changing body of knowledge.

We are indebted to many people for helping us understand how to create and deploy an effective predictive business analytics capability. We have learned from and been inspired by clients and colleagues and to each of you we express our gratitude for your insights and contributions.

We want to gratefully acknowledge the editorial support from Sheck Cho, Stacey Rivera, and Helen Cho, whose patience and guidance helped us create this book.

Lawrence S. Maisel
Gary Cokins
October 2013

NOTES

1. Kishore S. Swaminathan, "What the C-Suite Should Know about Analytics," *Accenture Outlook* 1, February 2011.
2. Predictive Analytics World survey, www.predictiveanalyticsworld.com/Predictive-Analytics-World-Survey-Report-Feb-2009.pdf.
3. Wayne Eckerson, "Predictive Analytics: Extending the Value of Your Data Warehousing Investment," TDWI Report.

4. David White, "Predictive Analytics: The Right Tool for Tough Times," an Aberdeen Group white paper, February 2010.

5. James Taylor and James Raden, *Smart (Enough) Systems: How to Deliver Competitive Advantage by Automating the Decisions Hidden in Your Business* (Upper Saddle River, NJ: Prentice Hall, 2007).

6. James Taylor, CEO and Principal Consultant, Decision Management Solutions, www.decisionmanagementsolutions.com.

7. The International Federation of Accountants (IFAC) and Lawrence S. Maisel have published an International Good Practice Guidance titled "Predictive Business Analytics: Forward-Looking Measures to Improve Business Performance," October 2011.

PART
ONE

"Why"

CHAPTER 1

Why Analytics Will Be the Next Competitive Edge

The farther backward you can look, the farther forward you are likely to see.

—Winston Churchill

A nalytics is becoming a competitive edge for organizations. Once a "nice to have," applying analytics, especially predictive business analytics, is now becoming mission-critical.

An August 6, 2009, *New York Times* article titled "For Today's Graduate, Just One Word: Statistics"[1] refers to the famous advice to Dustin Hoffman's character in his career-breakthrough movie *The Graduate*. The quote occurs when a self-righteous Los Angeles businessman takes aside the baby-faced Benjamin Braddock, played by Hoffman, and declares, "I just want to say one word to you—just one word—'plastics.'" Perhaps a remake of this movie will be made and updated with the word *analytics* substituted for *plastics*.

This spotlight on statistics is apparently relevant, because the article ranked in that week's top three e-mailed articles as tracked by the *New York Times*. The article cites an example of a Google employee who "uses statistical analysis of mounds of data to come up with ways to improve [Google's] search engine." It describes the employee as "an Internet-age statistician, one of many who are changing the image of the profession as a place for dronish number nerds. They are finding themselves increasingly in demand—and even cool."

ANALYTICS: JUST A SKILL, OR A PROFESSION?

The use of analytics that includes statistics is a skill that is gaining mainstream value due to the increasingly thinner margin for decision error. There is a requirement to gain insights, foresight, and inferences from the treasure chest of raw transactional data (both internal and external) that many organizations now store (and will continue to store) in a digital format.

Organizations are drowning in data but starving for information. The *New York Times* article states:

> In field after field, computing and the Web are creating new realms of data to explore—sensor signals, surveillance tapes, social network chatter, public records and more. And the digital data surge only promises to accelerate, rising fivefold by 2012, according to a projection by IDC, an IT research firm. . . . Yet data is merely the raw material of knowledge. We're rapidly entering a world where everything can be monitored and measured, but the big problem is going to be the ability of humans to use, analyze and make sense of the data. . . . [Analysts] use powerful computers and sophisticated mathematical models to hunt for meaningful patterns and insights in vast troves of data. The applications are as diverse as improving Internet search and online advertising, culling gene sequencing information for cancer research and analyzing sensor and location data to optimize the handling of food shipments.

An experienced analyst is like a caddy for a professional golfer. The best ones do not limit their advice to factors such as distance, slope, and the weather but also strongly suggest which club to use.

BUSINESS INTELLIGENCE VERSUS ANALYTICS VERSUS DECISIONS

Here is a useful way to differentiate business intelligence (BI) from analytics and decisions. Analytics simplify data to amplify its value. The power of analytics is to turn huge volumes of data into a much smaller amount of information and insight. BI mainly summarizes historical data, typically in table reports and graphs, as a means for queries and drill downs. But reports do not simplify data or amplify its value. They simply package up the data so it can be consumed.

In contrast to BI, decisions provide context for what to analyze. Work backward with the end decision in mind. Identify the decisions that matter most to your organization, and model what leads to making those decisions. If the type of decision needed is understood, then the type of analysis and its required source data can be defined.

Many believe that the use of BI software and creating cool graphs are the ultimate destination. BI is the shiny new toy of information technology. The reality is that much of what business intelligence software tools provide, as just described, has more to do with query and reporting, often by reformatting data. A common observation is: "There is no intelligence in business intelligence." It is only when data mining and analytics are applied to BI within an organization that has the skills, competencies, and capabilities that deep insights and foresight are created to understand the solutions to problems and select actions for improving business operations and opportunities.

Data mining that uses statistical methods is the foundation and precursor for predictive business analytics. For example, data mining can identify similar groups and segments (e.g., customers) through cluster or correlation analysis (see Chapter 4). This allows analysts to frame their analytics to predict how their objects of interest, such as customers, new medicines, new smartphones, and so on, are likely to behave in the future—with or without interventions. This allows predictive analytics to move from being *descriptive* to being *prescriptive*.

To clarify, BI consumes stored information. Analytics produces *new* information. Predictive business analytics leverages data within an organizational function focused on analytics and possessing the mandate, skills, and competencies to drive better decisions faster, and to achieve targeted performance.

Queries using BI tools simply answer basic questions. Business analytics creates questions. Further, analytics then stimulates more questions, more complex questions, and more interesting questions. More importantly, business analytics also has the power to *answer* the questions. Finally, predictive business analytics displays the probability of outcomes based on the assumptions of variables.

The application of analytics was once the domain of quants and statistical geeks developing models in their cubicles. However, today it is becoming mainstream for organizations with the conviction that senior executives will realize and utilize its potential value.

HOW DO EXECUTIVES AND MANAGERS MATURE IN APPLYING ACCEPTED METHODS?

Here is an observation on how managers mature in applying progressive managerial methods. Roughly 50 years ago, CEOs hired accountants to do the financial analysis of a company, because this was too complex for them to fully grasp. Today, all CEOs and businesspeople know what price-earnings (P/E) ratios and cash flow statements are and that they are essential to interpreting a business's financial health. These executives would not survive or get the job without this knowledge.

Fast-forward from then to 25 years ago, when many company CEOs did not have computers on their desks. They did not have the time or skill to operate these complex machines and applications, so they had their staff do this for them. Today you will become obsolete if you do not at least personally possess multiple electronic devices such as laptops, mobile phones, tablets, and personal digital assistants (PDAs) to have the information you need at your fingertips.

FILL IN THE BLANKS: WHICH X IS MOST LIKELY TO Y?

Predictive business analytics (PBA) allows organizations to make decisions and take actions they could not do (or do well) without analytics capabilities. Consider three examples:

1. **Increased employee retention.** Which of our employees will be the most likely next employee to resign and take a job with another company? By examining the traits and characteristics

of employees who have voluntarily left (e.g., age, time period between salary raises, percent wage raise, years with the organization), predictive business analytics can layer these patterns on the existing workforce. The result is a rank-order listing of employees most likely to leave and the reasons why. This allows managements' selective intervention.

2. **Increased customer profitability.** Which customer will generate the most profit from our least effort? By understanding various types of customers with segmentation analysis based on data about them (perhaps using activity-based costing as a foundational analysis), business analytics can answer how much can optimally be spent retaining, growing, winning back, and acquiring the attractive microsegment types of customers that are desired.

3. **Increased product shelf opportunity.** Which product in a retail store chain can generate the most profit without carrying excess inventory but also not having periods of stock-outs? By integrating sales forecasts with actual near-real-time point-of-sale checkout register data, predictive business analytics can optimize distribution cost economics with dynamic pricing to optimize product availability with accelerated sales throughput to maximize profit margins.

These three examples are fill-in-the-blanks questions. One can think of hundreds of others where the goal is to maximize or optimize actions or decisions. With predictive business analytics, the best and correct decisions can be made and organizational performance can be tightly monitored and continuously improved. Without predictive business analytics, an organization operates on gut feel and intuition, and optimization cannot even be in that organization's vocabulary.

PREDICTIVE BUSINESS ANALYTICS AND DECISION MANAGEMENT

Much is being written today about big data. Big data has been defined as a collection of data sets so large and complex that it becomes difficult to process using on-hand database management tools or traditional data processing applications. The challenges include capture, validation, storage, search, sharing, analysis, and visualization. What is needed is to shift the discussion from big data to big value. Business analytics and its amplifier, predictive business analytics, serve as a means to an end, and that end is faster, smarter decisions. Many may assume that this implies executive decisions, but the higher value for and benefit from applying analytics is arguably for daily operational decisions. Here is why.

Decisions can be segmented in three layers:

1. *Strategic decisions* are few in number but can have large impacts. For example, should we acquire a company or exit a market?
2. *Tactical decisions* involve controlling with moderate impacts. For example, should we modify our supply chain?
3. *Operational decisions* occur daily, even hourly, and often affect a single transaction or customer. For example, what deal should I offer to this customer or should I accept making this bank loan?

There are several reasons that operational decisions are arguably most important for embracing analytics. First, executing the executive team's strategy is not accomplished solely with strategy maps and their resulting key performance indicators (KPIs) in a performance scorecard and dashboards. The daily decisions are what actually move the dials. Next, although much is now written about enterprise risk management, the reality is that an organization's exposure to risk does not come in big chunks. Enterprise risk management deals more with reporting. Risk is incurred one event or transaction at a time. Finally, in the sales and marketing functions, operational decisions maximize customer value much more than do policies. For example, what should a frontline customer-facing worker do or say to a customer to gain profit lift? (Chapter 6 describes MetLife's journey to better decision management.) Operational decisions scale from the bottom up, and in the aggregate they can collectively exceed the impact of a few strategic decisions.

The baseball book (by Michael Lewis) and movie *Moneyball* highlighted the use of quantitative analysis to maximize results for the Oakland Athletics baseball team. But what many viewers, including enthusiastic analysts, did not realize is that the statistics were used in two steps with the larger payoff in the second step. First, the statistical analysis identified which mix of lower-salaried players to acquire and trade away. But after completing that step, the team still lost games. It was not until the next step that the team educated and trained each ballplayer at the pitch-by-pitch and play situation level and the Athletics began winning games. The second step is comparable to operational decisions. Good decisions add up to achieve the enterprise's goal— execute the strategy.

PREDICTIVE BUSINESS ANALYTICS: THE NEXT "NEW" WAVE

Today many businesspeople do not really know what predictive modeling, forecasting, design of experiments, and mathematical optimization mean or do, but over the next 10 years, use of these powerful techniques will become mainstream, just as financial analysis and computers have, if businesses want to thrive in a highly competitive and regulated marketplace. Executives, managers, and employee teams who do not understand, interpret, and leverage these assets will be challenged to survive.

When we look at what kids are learning in school, then that is certainly true. We were all taught mean, mode, range, and probability theory in our first-year university statistical analytics course. Today children have already learned these in the third grade! They are taught these methods in a very practical way. If you had x dimes, y quarters, and z nickels in your pocket, what is the chance of you pulling a dime from your pocket? Learning about range, mode, median, interpolation, and extrapolation follow in short succession. We are already seeing the impact of this with Gen Y/Echo Boomers who are getting ready to enter the workforce—they are used to having easy access to information and are highly self-sufficient in understanding its utility. The next generation after that will not have any fear of analytics or look toward an expert to do the math.

There is always risk when decisions are made based on intuition, gut feel, flawed and misleading data, or politics. In the popular book by Tom Davenport and Jeanne Harris *Competing on Analytics: The New Science of Winning*,[2] the authors make the case that increasingly the primary source of attaining a competitive advantage will be an organization's competence in mastering all flavors of analytics. If your management team is analytics-impaired, then your organization is at risk. Predictive business analytics is arguably the next wave for organizations to successfully compete and not only to predict outcomes but reach higher to optimize the use of their resources, assets, and trading partners, among other things.

It may be that the ultimate sustainable business strategy is to foster analytical competency and eventual mastery among an organization's workforce. Today managers and employee teams do not need a doctorate in statistics to investigate data and gain insights. Commercial software tools are designed for the casual user. Anyone can be chic.

GAME-CHANGER WAVE: AUTOMATED DECISION-BASED MANAGEMENT

What is the next big wave that will follow after analytics? Automated decision-based management. As organizations achieve competency and mastery with analytics, then the next step will be automated rules based on the outcomes from applying analytics. The islands of analytics emerging in an organization's various departments and processes will be unified in closed-loop ways. Communications will be in real time.

This does not mean that an organization's workforce will be reduced in size by robotlike decision making. But it does mean that algorithms, equations, and business rules derived from superior analysis will become essential to managing toward optimization. Decision-based managerial software will eventually emerge that is independent of but integrated with an organization's multitude of data storage platforms and data management stacks between the data and decisions. This future software's decisions will be aligned with the executive team's strategy and its key performance indicators. When that day comes, it will be a game-changer and the basis for a book to be written in the future.

Substantial benefits are realized from applying a systematic exploration of quantitative relationships among performance management factors. When the primary factors that drive an organization's success are measured, closely monitored, and predicted, that organization is in a much better situation to adjust, advance, and mitigate risks. That is, if a company is able to know—not just guess—which nonfinancial performance variables directly influence financial results, then it has a leg up on its competitors and delivers real value to its shareholders, employees, and other stakeholders.

PRECONCEPTION BIAS

Weak leaders are prone to a preconception bias. They can be blind to evidence and somehow believe their intuition, instincts, and gut feel are acceptable masquerades for having fact-based information.

Psychologists refer to this as a confirmation bias. What often trips managers up is they do not start by framing a problem before beginning to collect information that will lead to their conclusions. They often subconsciously start with a preconception. That is, they seek data that will validate their bias. The adverse effect is they prepare themselves for X, and Y is actually happening! By framing a problem and considering alternative points of view, one widens the options to formulate hypotheses. And this is where the emerging discipline of analytics fits in. With fact-based information, organizations gain insights and views that they might otherwise have missed.

Mental shortcuts, gut feel, intuition, and so on typically work *except* when problems get complex. When problems or opportunities get complex, then a new set of issues arises. Systematic thinking and application of analytics are required.

In the book *Analytics at Work: Smarter Decisions, Better Results,*[3] the authors note that 40 percent of important decisions are not based on facts but rather on intuition, experience, and anecdotal evidence. An immediate impression is that this is so sad. However, one ideology can take the position that perhaps intuition and experience are reliable for decisions—if the decision maker has exceptional intuition and experience. But intuition and experience are prerequisites. What if they don't sufficiently exist? Just look at the 2008 global economic meltdown. There were many smart minds managing the global economy. And look at what happened.

ANALYSTS' IMAGINATION SPARKS CREATIVITY AND PRODUCES CONFIDENCE

In contrast, curious people (curiosity is a trait of analysts) always ask questions. They query data to answer questions, and then use analytics to ask further and more robust questions. And better yet, their analytics can answer their questions. Analysts typically love what they do. If they are good with analytics, they infect others with enthusiasm. Their curiosity leads to imagination. Imagination considers alternative possibilities and solutions. Imagination in turn sparks creativity.

Once analysts produce results, they provide an important ingredient needed by decision makers—confidence. Confidence is a feeling and belief that one can rely on someone or something to make a decision and perform at some known time in the future. Effective analysts create confidence and trust with their stakeholders.

BEING WRONG VERSUS BEING CONFUSED

Which is worse—being wrong or being confused?

Let us start with some definitions. To make a wrong decision means you were mistaken and erroneous. Your decision was incorrect for the problem to be solved or opportunity that could have been realized (there is also an immoral, unethical, and illegal connotation; but that is a different variation of a poor choice). To be confused means you are baffled, bewildered, and perplexed. You cannot be positioned to make a correct decision because your thinking is muddled and clouded.

Embracing analytics can resolve both conditions.

Cultural Issues Related to Wrong Choices

An example of being wrong might be if you purchased a large top-loading clothes washing machine that did not fit in the space that a traditional front-loading washer would have fit in. Using the same example, being confused would be if you did not understand the differences between the two types of washers in terms of benefits, water consumption rates, and so on; you would then typically postpone the decision.

Postponing a decision when confused reduces the risk and possibly the embarrassment of making a mistake, but it also can mean missing the opportunity to be gained. Both involve risks. Different cultures approach risk in different ways.

Geert Hofstede, a Dutch researcher in social psychology, has done provocative research about Eastern versus Western culture's attitudes toward risk that sheds light on multicultural differences with risk appetite and decision making. In his book, *Culture's Consequences: Comparing Values, Behaviors, Institutions and Organizations across Nations*,[4] one of Hofstede's studies developed an Uncertainty Avoidance Index (UAI) that measures a nation's (or a society's or organization's) tolerance for uncertainty and ambiguity—its appetite for risk.

To abbreviate the details of the study's findings, it is convenient to describe two countries with cultures representing opposite and extreme ends of the UAI continuum. By better understanding these contrasting behavioral differences, project champions striving to successfully deploy predictive business analytics may better succeed. In Hofstede's study, UAI scores can range from 0 (pure risk takers—such as casino gamblers) to 100 (pure risk avoiders—very cautious and conservative). Of all the nations, the United States ranked lowest, implying fewer rules, fewer attempts to control outcomes, and greater tolerance for a variety of ideas, thoughts, and beliefs. In contrast, Japan ranked highest in its UAI score, implying high levels of control in order to eliminate or avoid the unexpected. A type of culture such as Japan's does not readily accept change and is risk averse.

Is Your Decision Making an Eastern or Western Type?

How can UAI apply to managing organizations? We believe there are obstacles and barriers that slow the adoption rate of predictive business analytics. They are no longer technical ones but rather involve people, culture, and human nature's resistance to change (see Chapter 5).

How would you personally assess the UAI of the organization you are employed by or one you keep an eye on or are involved with? Does it have a low UAI (U.S.-like)? This implies having self-concerned employees, less conformity, reliance on intuition and gut feel to wing it, avoiding rigid rules, low acceptance of authority, low trust levels, and reasonable tolerance for conflict, tension, and dissent.

In contrast, is your organization at the other extreme, with a high UAI (Japan-like)? This implies being collectivist with a need for consensus, being very analytical, and having more conformity, strict and enforced rules, high acceptance of authority, high levels of trust, and little tolerance for conflict. In Chapter 4, we present a method to rank and rate choices and calculate a value score that reflects these cultural biases as well as management priorities.

Implications for Success with Analytics

Ultimately all organizations will need to create a culture for analytics and fact-based decision making. Regardless of an organization's type of culture, what this all means is we must elevate the importance of organizational change management and behavior modification. Inevitably we will need to learn change management as on-the-job training.

So which is worse—being wrong or being confused? They are both bad with adverse consequences. Why not be smarter and safer at the same time?

AMBIGUITY AND UNCERTAINTY ARE YOUR FRIENDS

On the other side of the wrong versus confused coin is the notion that ambiguity and uncertainty are your friends. Suppose you are a business analyst or are responsible for enterprise performance and risk management; then ambiguity and uncertainty are your friends. Why? If getting answers were easy, your salary would probably be lower!

Search for Surprises

Regardless of how analytics might be defined, there should be no argument about what its purpose is—better insights and better decisions. If we take this reasoning further, we realize that analytics has much to do with problem solving and testing. It is about investigation and discovery.

University accounting faculty involved with teaching students and doing research make presentations, mainly research papers that can be stimulating. Some topics are a bit esoteric, such as "the role of persistent information asymmetry and learning by doing," but there are always a few golden nuggets. For example, at a managerial accounting conference, one presentation proved that in charitable fund-raising, the announcement of a wealthy donor's matching grant substantially increases donations from others (no big surprise); however, counterintuitively, increases of the match from one-to-one to multiples of more than one have no effect.

That is an example of what analysts and researchers seek—surprises. Having a surprise is not essential. Typically, analysis simply confirms a hypothesis. But what drives analysts and researchers is to prove that just having a hunch or an intuition for decisions is not good enough. They know if you do not test something that may be intuitive, then certain others will continue to believe that it is untrue! If their hypothesis is confirmed, that is fine; but if the conclusion has surprises, then new knowledge has been uncovered.

Quest for the Truth

Make no mistake. The scholars who present at managerial accounting conferences are not financial accountants who produce external reports for investors, bankers, and regulatory agencies. These professionals have dedicated their lives to a combination of educating future CFOs and hypothesizing research and testing for results and conclusions. They explore social, economic, and political problems.

The younger faculty's career advances depend on demonstrating good research, and the older ones maintain respect from their peers by acting as "discussants" following each research paper's presentation. The latter role is basically to provide constructive criticism and describe how the research contributes to the body of knowledge.

Analytics not only proves or disproves hypothesis, but its truth-seeking tests can also reveal cause-and-effect relationships. Understanding causality serves for making better decisions. Ambiguity and uncertainty? The greater the extent to which they exist, then the more challenging is the problem for an analyst and researcher to undertake. They can be an analyst's best friends.

DO THE IMPORTANT STUFF FIRST—PREDICTIVE BUSINESS ANALYTICS

Many of our experiences are that organizations overplan and under-execute. Now, we are not against planning. To the contrary, most of us are big believers in planning, but only up to a point. How many meetings have you been in where after what seems like endless rambling you say to yourself, "Heck, let's just start doing it"?

Plans do not have to be excessively detailed. After all, once you start acting on a plan, things rarely go perfectly according to that plan. So you begin adjusting and redirecting. Few things are not dynamic, especially in today's volatile times. In *The Art of War* (an ancient Chinese military treatise attributed to Sun Tzu), the author thought that strategy was not planning in the sense of working through an established list, but rather that it requires quick and appropriate responses to changing conditions. Planning works in a controlled environment; but in a changing environment, competing plans collide, creating unexpected situations.

However, what is important is what you do before the planning. In our mind there are two prerequisites: (1) frame the problem or opportunity that the plan addresses, and (2) perform analysis.

1. **Framing.** Framing a problem is not an easy task, except for simple plans. For example, one decides to take an umbrella if the sky has dark clouds but not if it is sunny. Is one 100 percent sure? Perhaps not, but the degree of certainly is probably good enough for the umbrella decision. But do you know or just think you know? This example gives a glimpse of the limits of planning. Mental shortcuts, gut feel, intuition, and so on typically work except when problems get complex. When problems or opportunities get complex, then a new set of issues arises. Systematic thinking is required. What often trips people up is they do not start by framing a problem before they begin collecting information that will lead to their conclusions. There is often a bias or preconception. One seeks data that will validate

one's bias. The adverse effect is we prepare ourselves for X and Y happens. By framing a problem, one widens the options to formulate hypotheses.

2. **Analytics.** Ah, the term *hypothesis*. It is critical and requires analytics, the second prerequisite, to prove or disprove the validity of the hypothesis. Much is now being written about analytics. There is a reason. The margin for error keeps getting slimmer. Also, previously accepted types of strategies (e.g., low-cost producer) are vulnerable to competitor actions. The only truly sustainable strategy is to have organizational competency with analytics.

Our suggestion is to do the important stuff first. Frame, analyze, and then plan. But plan to replan—numerous times. Reliable forecasting and probabilistic scenario planning would be nice additions to your portfolio of analytics.

WHAT IF ... YOU CAN

Are you curious about why the following questions have not been solved? With predictive business analytics and enterprise performance management software, they can be!

- Why can't traffic intersection stoplights be more variable based on street sensors that monitor the presence, location, and speed of approaching vehicles? Then you would not have to impatiently wait at a red light when there is no cross traffic.

- Why can't a call center route your inbound phone call to a more specialized call center representative based on your phone number and previous call topics or transactions? And once connected, why can't that call rep offer you rule-based deals or suggestions most likely to maximize your customer experience? Then you might get a quicker and better solution to your call.

- Why can't dentists and doctors synchronize patient appointment schedule arrival times to reduce the amount of time so many people collectively sit idly in their waiting rooms? Then you could show up just before your treatment.

- Why can't airlines better alert their ground crews for plane gate arrivals? Then you wouldn't have to wait, sometimes endlessly, for the jet bridge crew to show up and open the door.

- Why can't hotel elevators better position the floors the elevators arrive at to pick up passengers based on when hotel guests depart their rooms? Then you wouldn't have to get stuck on a slow "milk-run" elevator stopping at so many floors while an express elevator that subsequently arrived could have quickly taken you to your selected floor.

- Why can't airport passport control managers regulate the number of agents in synchronization with the arrivals of international flights? Then you wouldn't have to wait in long queues and then later the extra staff shows up (sometimes).

- Why can't retail stores partner with credit card companies and their transaction histories and use algorithms like Amazon.com and Netflix use to suggest what a customer might want? Then you might more quickly find what you are shopping for.

- Why can't water, gas, and electrical utility suppliers to home residences provide instant monitoring and feedback so that households can determine which appliances or events (e.g., taking showers) consume relatively more or less energy? Then households could adjust their usage behavior to better manage cost and energy consumption.

- Why can't personnel and human resource departments do better workforce planning on both the demand side and the supply side? That is, for the supply side, why can't they predict in rank order the most likely next employee to resign or, based on statistical data (e.g., age, pay raise amount, or frequency), the number of employees who have resigned? For those who will retire, isn't this predictable? For the demand side, why can't improved forecasting of sales volume be translated into head count capacity planning by type of skill or job group? Then the workforce would match the needs without scrambling when mismatches occur.

- Why can't magazines you subscribe to print at the time of production a customized issue to you that has advertisements (and maybe even articles) that you likely care more about based on whatever profile they may have about you? Then the magazine's content may be more relevant to you.

- Why can't your home's refrigerator and pantry keep track using microchips and barcode scanners of what you purchased and the rate of usage? Then you could better replenish your food supplies when out shopping.

Are these visions of the future? Not in all cases. With predictive business analytics, some if not all of these questions are already solvable. It is time that gut feel, intuition, and guessing be replaced with applying predictive business analytics to better manage organizations and better serve their customers.

NOTES

1. "For Today's Graduate, Just One Word: Statistics," the *New York Times*, available at www.nytimes.com/2009/08/06/technology/06stats.html?scp=1&sq=Graduate%20 statistics&st=cse.

2. Thomas H. Davenport and Jeanne G. Harris, *Competing on Analytics: The New Science of Winning* (Boston: Harvard Business School Publishing, 2007).

3. Thomas H. Davenport, Robert Morison, and Jeanne G. Harris, *Analytics at Work: Smarter Decisions, Better Results* (Boston: Harvard Business School Publishing, 2010).

4. Geert Hofstede, *Culture's Consequences: Comparing Values, Behaviors, Institutions and Organizations across Nations* (Thousand Oaks, CA: Sage, 2001).

CHAPTER **2**

The Predictive Business Analytics Model

It is not the strongest of the species that survives, nor the most intelligent, but the one most responsive to change.

—Charles Darwin

"Apple's Steve Jobs was known to explicitly discount the value of surveys and focus groups for designing new products. How do you explain this apparent anti-empiricism? One explanation is that, much like a creative scientist, people like Jobs recognize when there is not enough data or the right kind of data to form a theory. They recognize that, for completely new lines of products that will change a user's experience or behavior, the only useful data is experiential data, not commentary and reactions from those who have never used the product.

This approach to decision making using empiricism and analytics might seem like a death knell for such vaunted business traits as intuition, gut feel, killer instinct, and so forth, right? Not so fast! Business decision making can be purely empirical and dispassionate, but decision makers are not. Sound decision making favors those who are creative, are intuitive, and can take a leap of faith.

Data, by itself, can be interpreted in many ways. Imagine a physical or business phenomenon that produces the following sequence of data: 1, 2, 6, 24, 33. Perhaps it is a factorial sequence with 33 as noise, or perhaps every fifth term is the sum of the previous four. Both are indeed correct. To prove or disprove either theory, you need the next several terms of the sequence. A good scientist knows when there is enough data to warrant a theory, when there is not, what new data to gather, and how to design an experiment to gather the right data.

The enterprise of the future, based on empiricism and analytical decision making, will indeed be considerably different from today's enterprise. You may well ask: "Do you think this is true, or do you know?"[1]

Today, more than ever, businesses are expected to possess the talent, tools, processes, and capabilities to enable their organizations to implement and utilize continuous analysis of past business performance and events to gain forward-looking insight to drive business decisions and actions. More and more organizations are seeking better processes and tools to ensure that the right people have the right information at the right time, to make smarter decisions. To promote clarity and ensure that the application of predictive analytics is relevant to all organizational functions, we have elected to use the term *predictive business analytics* (PBA). This process, in essence, reflects an organizational capability to improve managerial decision making across many core performance areas. For years, organizations have sought to develop and deploy an effective process to capture and filter forward-looking measures that enable it to understand significant patterns, relationships, and trends in order to facilitate better and more insightful decisions about the future. Several terms are in current use for this process: predictive analytics, business analysis, driver-based forecasting, and so on. While these terms and their underlying methodologies are valuable, they are still techniques of "how to do these actions." PBA is the organization function and capability within which these techniques are applied, interpreted, and communicated among key constituents whose roles and responsibilities are planned and executed using such critical information and insights.

As the term implies, PBA is forward-looking in nature and based on analysis of relevant business data and drivers that have a strong and traceable linkage to financial results and operational performance. Business drivers can be financial or operational; they can also be external or internal. There are many examples of such drivers: (1) some reflect changes over time, such as new home sales, new product sales, mortgage delinquencies, and foreclosures; (2) some reflect changes in a given period, such as new births, new car sales, and new hirings; and (3) some reflect changes at a point in time, such as changes in interest rates, fuel prices, tax rates, and sales commissions. PBA should enable management to identify new opportunities for growth and improvement, as well as to highlight areas for corrective actions and possibly strategy adaptations.

These past several years of economic turbulence and uncertainty have provided excellent examples of the importance and benefits to be realized by organizations that have developed a workable PBA process and used it to anticipate and guide its operations to productive outcomes. Conversely, that period also demonstrated the consequences of omitting or not adequately developing a relevant PBA process. "Analytics has been around for a long time and generally refers to the process of using decision-support systems, business intelligence, statistics, and predictive models to give companies a competitive edge and is used by high-performing companies to improve profitability."[2]

A recent survey of over 400 senior financial leaders in both the public and private sectors found that high-performing companies outperformed low performers by 54 percent in several key categories, and were 43 percent more effective in their use of alerts or warning systems, driver-based forecasting, and data mining. This enabled them to manage by exception and be proactive, rather than be reactive to emerging issues and opportunities. High performers were also 44 percent more effective in "cascading" accountability for business drivers through the use of relevant and controllable performance metrics.[3] One of the more effective performance reporting tools is the performance scorecard, which, if done properly, provides a line of sight to key performance indicators (KPIs). These KPIs provide a causal relationship among drivers and outcomes to strategies, operational processes, and key business initiatives.

Recently, there have been some misconceptions between PBA and other forms of business intelligence. Business intelligence traditionally focuses on using a consistent set of metrics both to measure past performance and to guide business planning, which is also based on data and statistical methods. Additionally, data mining, sometimes referred to as predictive analytics or "Big Data", focuses on consumer behaviors and patterns. Business intelligence is querying and reporting. These capabilities such as querying, reporting, online analytical processing (OLAP), and alert tools answer only questions such as what happened, how many, how often, where the problem is, and what actions are needed. PBA can answer questions like why this is happening, what if these trends continue, what will happen next, what is the best that can happen, and (most important) what we can learn and what actions or adaptations, if any, we should take.

Let us compare the use of predictive business analytics in driving fact-based decisions to that of the human experience. This whole notion functions like the human experience; you understand it with your brain, in your heart you believe it, and in your body you actually execute it. And I think that is a little bit how predictive business analytics works, in that as there is more confidence within the organization in the insight of the cause-and-effect relationships (the brain, if you will) that the organization will come to believe and trust (the heart), and then the actual organizational structures and operations will begin to execute it (the muscles). That kind of parallels the human experience. The body will not do what the mind does not drive it to do. And the mind will drive it only if it believes it and understands it.

Now that we know what PBA is and what are some of its benefits, the next step is to define how we go about implementing it. It has been my experience that an effective way to get started is to adhere to a set of principles that can guide how the PBA capability can be embedded into the organization.

The International Federation of Accountants (IFAC)[4] has published a set of guiding principles for PBA that are intended to be globally adopted. These are described in detail in Chapter 3; a summary of these guiding principles follows:

- **Demonstrate a strong *cause-and-effect* relationship.** In order to be able to predict outcomes, it is important to measure and monitor what drivers or events most likely cause the outcome(s) to occur.

- **Contain a *balanced* set of financial and nonfinancial, internal and external measures.** Too often management reporting is concentrated on internally focused financial results, like net income, and less on the nonfinancial activities that have a financial impact or on externally driven metrics that show how the marketplace views the organization.
- **Be *relevant, reliable,* and *timely* for decision makers.** PBA should be provided to users when, where, and how they need it. Analytics should be relevant to the business, industry, or function. It must have the right level of timeliness and reliability to the critical issues being addressed. In other words, it is "fit for purpose."
- **Ensure data *integrity*.** Data integrity is of paramount importance and should be supported by an organization's ability to establish data standards and data quality practices, which is the foundation for a trusted and accepted PBA.
- **Be *accessible* and well *organized*.** For PBA to contribute to managerial decisions and actions, it needs to be easily accessible using tools and technologies that are user-friendly and organized in a way that reflects the business model.
- **Integrate into the *management* process.** PBA and forward-looking performance measures should be tied to accountabilities, be linked to operating results and performance, and be an integral part of the management review process.
- **Drive *behaviors* and *results*.** PBA should highlight those measures that foster desired behaviors of the organization such as innovation, teamwork, collaboration, risk taking, and so forth. Accordingly, it is important that PBA is tied to reward and recognition processes.

The primary purpose of PBA is to identify how the future might look and what subsequent actions need to be taken. It is a continuous process to cultivate managerial and operational decision making that affects future financial and operating results and facilitates strategy execution. Several uses of this process include:

- Updating forecasts of projected results given the current state.
- Evaluating changes to current strategies and operating plans (deviations) and adopting corrective actions (gap closing).

- Sharing expectations among interdependent groups or entities.
- Looking around the curve with an eye toward actions and changes.
- Approximating results based on changes in business drivers to provide a broad palette of alternative actions for discussion and decision by responsible managers.

PBA supports an organization's need for a capability to anticipate future events, forecast their possible outcomes, and select actions and decisions that affect its business results, operational capabilities, response to changing market and industry dynamics, and recruitment and retention of critical people, skills, and competencies. The use of PBAs can be illustrated with an example from a consumer finance company.

A consumer finance company monitors its outstanding credit card balances across several key internal and external attributes. Internal attributes include aging of balances, level of repayments relative to minimums due, geographies, and demographics, to name a few. In addition, external attributes include employment rates, unemployment insurance claims, credit scores, and so forth. These attributes or drivers form the foundation of an organization's ability to apply PBA to its business model and to convert its insight into a series of decisions and actions. Several critical elements are necessary to make this process relevant:

- Information quality (e.g., Is the data trustworthy? Are the relationships causal and consistent?).
- Tools and access to the information (e.g., Are formats graphic and intuitive? Is information easily and rapidly accessible?).
- Operating processes to capture, validate, distribute, and analyze relevant data for establishing performance insights and facilitating decisions at the designated levels of accountability.
- Skilled individuals knowledgeable and informed about the strategic or operational results and their implications (e.g., What happened? vs. Why is it happening?, Is this an anomaly or is it a trend? If it is a trend, will the trend continue?).
- Credible management processes in place to raise awareness and determine actions and decisions, and a process to monitor and measure the effectiveness of these actions.

BUILDING THE BUSINESS CASE FOR PREDICTIVE BUSINESS ANALYTICS

According to an IBM/MIT *Sloan Management Review* study, "Analytics: The New Path to Value, "the adoption barriers organizations face most are related to management and culture rather than data and technology. The leading obstacle to widespread analytics adoption is lack of understanding on how to use analytics to improve business according to almost 40% of respondents. More than one in three cite lack of management bandwidth due to company priorities."[5]

A well-structured and properly executed PBA program can achieve tangible and measurable benefits in a variety of core performance areas (see sidebar).

CORE PERFORMANCE AREAS

Economic. Are we optimizing revenues by anticipating future events and market trends? Are we eliminating or avoiding non-value-added costs of services, financing, and so on? In effect, are we delivering the results and value expected by our key stakeholders (e.g., shareholders, creditors, customers, employees)?

Strategic. Are we positioned for future changes to our functional and industry practices, opportunities, and competitors? Can we recognize and respond rapidly to fundamental changes in our business model, customer markets, competitive positions, regulatory requirements, and external developments?

Operational. Are we using and managing the proper operating business model for our customers, suppliers, employees, stakeholders, and regulators? Are we achieving the proper balance of effectiveness and efficiency? Are our governance, risk management, and control practices and policies meaningfully related to how we operate and perform?

Technological. Are our use of technologies relevant and appropriate for our business model? Do our people have the tools to be aware, productive, and effective? Have we captured, stored, and accessed data and converted into actionable insights and decisions? Does our technologies enable us to be more competitive?

Organizational and Reputational. Are we sufficiently transparent in our management processes? Do we have the right set of skills, competences, and resource capabilities? Are our people and colleagues treated fairly? Are rewards and recognition systems effective in incentivizing desired behaviors and performance cultures? Do we recognize our societal obligations for the environment, and the sustainability of our owned and used natural resources? Do we comply with defined laws and regulations and our internally stated values and code of conduct?

Although PBA may not necessarily be a management methodology, it is a broader extension of such existing tools and techniques such as the performance or balanced scorecard, forecasting, and target setting, to name a few. It requires knowledge and understanding of the activities across the organization to determine measures across all functions and how they interrelate, in order to begin to predict patterns and behaviors that ultimately have a financial impact.

The quality of management information expected by internal business users is expanding both in terms of the range of data to be considered and the level of required analysis. From strategic issues to routine tasks, all executives, managers, and operational staff expect higher-quality information to support their decision making. Management information should also (1) relate financial to nonfinancial performance measures, (2) report past performance and monitor current operations, and (3) assist operating managers to anticipate future events and, if needed, take appropriate corrective actions.

BUSINESS PARTNER ROLE AND CONTRIBUTIONS

The perception of the PBA business partner is that of an individual or a designated function within an organization that will provide analytical support to decision makers and others. These professionals are increasingly expected to have the capacity to provide decision support to organizational leaders and managers with information and analysis about the organization's position and course. They contribute to strategic and operational decision making, and are prepared, when necessary, to challenge constructively to ensure that the organization is managed in the long-term interests of stakeholders. In essence, these professionals need to contribute, basing that contribution on hard analytics and facts, to earn their reputation as valued business partners to the organization.

SUMMARY

In this chapter, we described the predictive business analytics model and the organization function and capability within which traditional analysis techniques are applied, interpreted, and communicated among key constituents whose roles and responsibilities are planned and executed using such critical information and insights.

The primary purpose of PBA is to identify how the future might look and what subsequent actions need to be taken. It is a continuous process to cultivate managerial and operational decision making that affects future financial and operating results and facilitates strategy execution.

As the term implies, PBA is forward-looking in nature, oriented to the organization at an enterprise level, and based on analysis of relevant business data and drivers that have a strong and traceable linkage to financial results and operational performance. Business drivers can be financial or operational; they can also be external or internal.

The chapter concludes by highlighting the business partner role and its contributions to improving decision making and operating performance.

NOTES

1. Kishore S. Swaminathan, "What the C-Suite Should Know about Analytics," *Accenture Outlook* 1, February 2011.
2. Marie Leone, "All the Right Data," CFO.com, quoting Jeanne Harris, February 2, 2010, www.cfo.com/article.cfm/14473223/c_14473073.
3. PricewaterhouseCoopers, LLP, "Performance Management Matters: Sustaining Superior Results in a Global Economy," June 2009, 2, www.pwc.com/ca/en/finance/performance-management/global-performance-management-research-study.jhtml.
4. The International Federation of Accountants (IFAC) and Lawrence S. Maisel have published an International Good Practice Guidance titled "Predictive Business Analytics: Forward-Looking Measures to Improve Business Performance," October 2011.
5. "Analytics: The New Path to Value," a joint study published by IBM's Institute for Business Value and MIT's *Sloan Management Review*, 2010.

PART
TWO

Principles and Practices

CHAPTER **3**

Guiding Principles in Developing Predictive Business Analytics

You miss 100 percent of the shots you never take.

—Wayne Gretzky

In the evolution of meaningful management practices, a few fundamental characteristics have emerged, one of which is the ability to define a sustaining and relevant set of guiding principles. These principles can be either principle-based or rule-based. Principle-based ones are those that provide insight and also leave room for sound business judgments and adaptations, such as macroeconomic theory or laws of aerodynamics. Rule-based ones are those that set forth clear standards with little room for broad interpretations, such as the U.S. tax code or the U.S. Golf Association's Rules of Golf (although some do try to reinterpret those rules).

One of the first and critically important steps in developing a predicative business analytics (PBA) function and capability is to define a set of guiding principles and to obtain the organization's concurrence regarding these principles. It is not uncommon that an organization will view this process as too tightly structured around functional departments. If I am in sales and marketing, what I see is sales and marketing. I may not see inventory and often do not see manufacturing as an issue because I am so focused on my individual function. As a result, insights from cross-functional data and actions might drop into the proverbial black hole.

Consequently, a critical initial step in organizing and deploying a contributing PBA function is to establish a set of guiding principles. These are defined within the context of the company's management practices (i.e., governance and decision authorities, data access and quality) and structures (i.e., reporting relationships, span of control, decentralization), including its reward and recognition systems. In later chapters we discuss designing the PBA function (Chapter 4) and implementing the PBA capability (Chapter 5) and organizational challenges and change management issues (Chapter 13).

DEFINING A RELEVANT SET OF PRINCIPLES

Seven guiding principles have been defined that follow the notion of a principles-based approach, which is essential to developing and sustaining a robust and meaningful predictive business analytics capability within a company. These principles are intended to guide its leadership team to harvest the competitive benefits and rewards that PBA is capable of delivering to the organization.

Each principle is defined and described in the following pages. The order is not important. What is important is that these are deployed as an integrated set for achieving the most effective functional capabilities and successes.

PRINCIPLE 1: DEMONSTRATE A STRONG *CAUSE-AND-EFFECT* RELATIONSHIP

Causality is the relationship between an event (the cause or driver) and a second event (the effect or outcome), where the second event is a consequence of the first. To successfully predict outcomes, it is important to understand the cause-and-effect relationship between events (their drivers). The key question is: "If this happens, then what will happen as a result?" Simple cause-and-effect examples include: If head count goes up, so will costs; or, if shipping errors increase, customer loyalty and ultimately revenue will decrease. In the development of medicines, the number of clinical data errors will slow down the clinical trial process and hence lengthen cycle time, and ultimately delay launch and anticipated revenues. Effective portrayal of cause-and-effect performance measures enhances the ability to predict outcomes. In a predictive model, the technique of back-testing the cause-and-effect relationships used in a predictive model can also help provide an insight into the effectiveness of the measures being used.

PBA should be able to reasonably predict future outcomes, and be based on provable causal linkages rather than best guesses. Every measure selected should be part of a chain of cause-and-effect relationships that represents and aligns the strategy, measures, targets, and initiatives of the organization. It can be common for process improvement efforts that focus on the inputs and outputs of a process to be able to quickly highlight the cause-and-effect relationship between inputs and outputs—otherwise referred to as process and results measures, and often referred to as leading (process) and lagging (results) measures. A process measure is one that can typically influence and change such things as cycle time or data errors. A results measure is often too late to enable changes to be made, such as in net income or earnings per share. The appropriate balance of process and results measures that show a cause-and-effect relationship will allow PBA to better predict outcomes.

The ability to make decisions based on PBA requires insight into the internal economics of an organization, which in turn requires information and analysis from the organization's costing system. An organization's capability to understand the cause-and-effect cycle from external drivers of change therefore needs to be linked to its internal processes and resources, which will ultimately drive costs and investments necessary to respond. An organization's PBA and costing system should be able to effectively analyze the impact of predictive scenarios so that potential operational impacts and responses are understood. The PBA process can directly address uncertainties and assumptions derived from a scenario planning process. See Chapter 10 for a more thorough discussion of marginal expense analytics.

PRINCIPLE 2: INCORPORATE A *BALANCED* SET OF FINANCIAL AND NONFINANCIAL, INTERNAL AND EXTERNAL MEASURES

Although organizations may have a significant amount of data, often only one or few measurements are focused on, which causes an unbalanced view of organizational performance. For product development, a core measure could be the number of innovations moved to a new stage of development. A salesperson may close a deal on an unprofitable sale, while product development may push a bad potential product forward. This clearly shows the need for balance and an ability to make choices. "If I sign this deal, my profit margins will suffer." Or "If I move this bad product forward for more development, we will spend more money on a product that will not result in revenue." A balanced set of measures helps in making decisions, particularly about trade-offs.

A balanced set of measures will reflect internal and external factors and drivers and incorporate financial and nonfinancial performance. The number of customer returns is a nonfinancial process measure that can indicate to managers a negative impact on revenue. Some nonfinancial measures can be sustainability related, such as carbon emissions. External measures indicate the projected economic climate, the marketplace environment, and the potential impact of competitors and suppliers. Business measures also referred to as drivers can be financial or operational; they can also be external or internal. There are many examples of such drivers: (1) some reflect changes over time, such as new home sales, new product sales, mortgage delinquencies, and foreclosures; (2) some reflect changes in a given period, such as new births, new car sales, and new hires; and (3) some reflect changes at a point in time, such as changes in interest rates, fuel prices, tax rates, and sales commissions. Drivers will typically be related to external uncertainties and factors that impact the competitive environment and the organization, such as changes in the competition, technology, consumer preferences and demand, as well as market changes. An organization's risk management can also feed into the PBA process as risk management explicitly takes account of uncertainty, the nature of that uncertainty, and how it can be addressed.

PRINCIPLE 3: BE *RELEVANT*, *RELIABLE*, AND *TIMELY* FOR DECISION MAKERS

For PBA to be of value, it should (1) reflect the relevance to business users, (2) be the result of a consistent and trusted process, and (3) reflect the appropriate time frame for the decisions being made. Users need meaningful data at the right time and in a form they can rely on. For PBA information to be meaningful, it should be tailored to the designated consumers of that information in a form and context that describes the outcomes, causes, and consequences of decisions and actions associated with alternative future drivers (amounts or quantities) and business conditions. Information should be presented in a manner that conveys the key messages and portrays the alternative actions in an unambiguous and straightforward manner, using formats that are graphic and intuitively understood. For example, in traveling to a business meeting, the driver sees a series of data points on an automobile dashboard (e.g., gauges for speed, engine temperature, oil pressure). These may be complete, but unless they inform the user of the range of acceptable tolerances and the implication related to the situation (e.g., highway versus bumpy country road), they will usually not be sufficient for meaningful decision making and actions about safety and timely arrival. Building on this example, PBA can be expanded to provide alerts and suggested alternative decisions and actions that might be considered.

Relevance

PBA should reflect an organization's business model and develop forward-looking information in a manner that facilitates focused decision making regarding relevant business issues and decisions. For example, a health care organization analyzing its staffing needs will likely gather data about its (1) service area population (e.g., age, ethnicity, gender) and (2) present and future health care reimbursement contracts and conditions. These attributes (and others) will enable the organization to better select the range of options regarding its longer-term staffing levels, competencies and skills requirements, and specialties, as well as service-level capacities (e.g., number of beds) in each of these specialty areas. The data from the analysis should be useful to the user or it will not be used. The tolerance of the ranges needs to be "fit for purpose." For example, predicting required production volumes by location for next week's operating plans and scheduling is different from predicting revenues six months forward. Asking users what decisions they want to make based on the data is a place to start to ensure the usefulness of the analysis.

Reliability

PBA should provide fit-for-purpose data to users when, where, and how they need it. Reliability often refers to predictability. If a process consistently produces the same outcome, it is said to be predictable. If a process never produces the same outcome, it cannot be relied on. For example, if a machine with the same settings never produces a unit of the same shape and length, it lacks reliability. The same holds for PBA. Although the analysis will vary, the output must be relied on to be useful to the users. The process by which the analysis is created should be standard and consistent. If users do not trust the performance measurement system, they will not use it.

Timeliness

Timely data is critical to the ability to predict outcomes. However, while information that is six months old may not be useful to the user, it may not be necessary to have daily or real-time information delivery.

PRINCIPLE 4: ENSURE DATA *INTEGRITY*

Integrity with respect to data is a concept of consistency of actions, values, methods, measures, principles, expectations, and outcomes. The source of the data for PBA should have integrity. Data integrity underlies an organization's efforts to establish data standards and data quality practices. Data integrity refers to the ability to trust the underlying data. Without trusted data, even the most consistent process will produce bad results.

All users of information derived from the PBA process should be made aware of data integrity and quality issues, or where (best) estimates of data input have been used. Underlying assumptions used in collecting and analyzing the data should be transparent. Data integrity and validity can also be tested in retrospect and the results communicated openly.

PRINCIPLE 5: BE *ACCESSIBLE*, UNDERSTANDABLE, AND WELL *ORGANIZED*

In PBA, all levels of the organization should use consistent data, analytical practices, and tools. This creates transparency by sharing one version of the truth with various management teams and users. Instead of discussing individually generated reports and forecasted analysis with different versions of the truth, managers need access to the same set of performance measures on which they can exercise their judgments. Different levels of users need different lenses to view management information and predictive measures. Accessibility contributes to transparency and operational synergies. For example, integrating data from R&D, engineering, and manufacturing could significantly reduce cycle time and improve quality.

There are user-friendly tools and technologies that are easy for the user to interact with and conducive to examining outcomes based on alternate driver values and possible business scenarios. These tools and technologies, when implemented correctly, greatly aid in establishing reliable and timely data while enhancing the level of confidence in the forward-looking outcomes that become the basis for decisions and actions. However, most predictions, no matter how carefully prepared, are to some extent uncertain. The way a prediction is presented and its limitations need to be disclosed to users.

PRINCIPLE 6: INTEGRATE INTO THE *MANAGEMENT* PROCESS

To become a trusted input into decision making, PBA and forward-looking performance measures should be tied to accountabilities and related to promotion or rewards, and thus be an integrated part of the management process. This involves developing roles and responsibilities accountabilities and governance structures and practices.

Roles and responsibilities should be clear, and incentives should be in place to (1) influence behaviors, (2) reinforce organizational alignments and management authorities, and (3) ensure coherent decision making. Accuracy of outcomes should be weighed against several factors in determining the effectiveness of management decision making, such as risk, resource requirements, and short-term versus long-term trade-offs.

PBA should establish a clear set of accountabilities and responsibilities for owning each step of a process. Responsibilities extend from capturing and validating financial and operational data to defining the decision-making authorities and accountabilities for actions within defined governance practices.

Governance practices related to PBA should be defined and disseminated. This should include defining roles and responsibilities, ownership for updating and reviewing data, and approval processes for making changes. To help implement such processes, charts can be used to specify and map the decisions and/or actions and, related to each decision or action, assign organizational positions and individuals who (1) initiate the action or decision, (2) approve the action or decision, (3) are informed about the action or decision, and (4) are consulted about the action or decision. Generally, the more detailed and specific the roles and authorities aligned to decisions and actions, the better the governance process. See Chapter 6 as an excellent example of integrating PBA into the management process.

PRINCIPLE 7: DRIVE *BEHAVIORS* AND *RESULTS*

The adage that "you get what you measure" holds true with PBA. Therefore, PBA should drive desired behaviors and results. If shortened cycle time is a desired outcome, then by measuring it, understanding and eliminating or reducing its drivers/causes, predicting it, and holding people accountable to cycle times will result in shortened cycle times. Benchmarking and rewards can also be effectively used to ensure that desired behaviors and results are achieved.

Benchmarking

Wherever possible, predictive performance measures should be compared to those of other internal groups or external competitors. Benchmarking information should be evaluated for its comparability and relevance to its prospective use. Benchmarking often highlights areas of needed improvement in cost, cycle times, and quality. Benchmarks in these areas can be used to rally organizations around needed improvements and efficiency gains.

Rewards

PBA should highlight those measures that foster desired behaviors to support the delivery of organizational objectives and intended results. Rewards and recognition might be used to foster desired behaviors of the organization, such as innovation, teamwork, and collaboration. Sometimes, the organization should reward and recognize risk-taking actions that have been approved, even if these fail, so as to promote that kind of culture of the organization. Performance-related remuneration should encourage the right behavioral triggers.

SUMMARY

In this chapter, we established a set of guiding principles that a reader can use to frame the design (Chapter 4) and deployment (Chapter 5) of a PBA function. These guiding principles are just that, principles, and not hard-and-fast rules. These are intended to guide an organization to foster its predictive business analytic capabilities and enable a leadership team to harvest the competitive benefits and rewards.

Each principle focuses on a specific element that, when taken as a whole and integrated into the PBA functional capabilities, yields a process that can be sustained and demonstrate its contributed value to the organization.

CHAPTER **4**

Developing a Predictive Business Analytics Function

Think of analytics as a toolbox. One screwdriver of a particular size and style isn't going to build you a chest of drawers—much less so in the hands of an inexperienced carpenter.

—John Lucker, "Business Analytics: Fad or Fundamental?,"
Deloitte Development LLC, 2012

Although some amount of predictive modeling can be done by means of pre-formed queries, pivot tables, summarized reports, and so on—that's just rudimentary. The ultimate value of all that data will only become evident if the people who know how to think about the data can access it easily, explore different views, test various hypotheses, and share their findings effectively.[1]

Many organizations have often introduced or at least recognize the need for an analytical capability to better understand how past events might influence future plans, shape decisions, and impact expected operating results. These organizations may develop specific applications or practices such as forecasting, scenario modeling, and contingent planning, to name a few, to address these analytical needs. While these tools and techniques address specific requirements, they can vary in terms of usefulness, relevance, and responsiveness.

In essence, what organizations are seeking is to make informed decisions based on the most current, relevant information available at the time. What distinguishes predictive business analytics (PBA) is that the decision-making process is rooted in a structured, continuous, and data-driven process that enables an organization to select actions with a fair degree of understanding of how these decisions and actions were determined and to have a reasonable level of confidence regarding outcomes and impacts.

An effective way to determine the need and potential benefits for developing a PBA capability is to assess the need according to your organization's level of maturity and capabilities. A simple but illustrative chart, Exhibit 4.1, allows you to gauge your organization's level of maturity and capabilities as a starting point to determining how to best structure a PBA function that is sustainable and will be viewed as a value contributor to your company's success.

Once you have gauged your organization's level of maturity and current capabilities, the next step is to set a direction. Our experience tells us that to best achieve success it is advisable to follow two concurrent paths to getting started. First, adopt a change management process, and second, envision a desired target state.

GETTING STARTED

> People change what they do less because they are given
> analysis that shifts their thinking than because they are
> shown a truth that influences their feelings.[2]

In John Kotter's landmark book on organizational change, *Leading Change*,[3] he described a process for effecting change in an organization. The art of starting a PBA process can leverage from his Eight-Stage Process of Creating Major Change (see Exhibit 4.2). This initial set of steps is particularly critical to achieving a solid start.

Exhibit 4.1 Predictive Business Analytics Maturity Capability Map

Stage	I	II	III	IV
Characteristics	**Traditional Analytics**	**Specific Events**	**Functional Silos**	**Integrated**
Process	▪ Reacts to ad hoc inquiries ▪ Reviews and decision making follow routine practices ▪ Gut feel	▪ One-off analysis of a specific event or transaction ▪ Team formed for purpose and disbands after completing analysis	▪ Established function but is limited to designated area of focus ▪ Informal interactions and sharing of results and data	▪ Well-developed process with established rules of governance and communications ▪ Track record of success
Data	▪ Historic and available ▪ Little validation of cause and effect ▪ Primarily internal and single data type	▪ Collecting available data on an ad hoc basis ▪ Purchased database or benchmark	▪ Fragmented and stored within functional area ▪ Limited awareness across organization ▪ Data-driven decisions	▪ Routinely captured and stored ▪ Tested for relevance and integrity ▪ Data-driven decisions
Tools	▪ Nonspecialized (e.g., MS Excel)	▪ Some level of analytical data mining software ▪ Some level of statistical modeling	▪ Some level of analytical data mining software ▪ Some level of statistical modeling	▪ Use of recognized tools for analytical purposes ▪ Adaptive to prior uses and future needs
Skills	▪ Nonspecialized generalist ▪ Subject matter expert as requested	▪ Skill contributed by team members and possible use of outside consultants/SMEs	▪ Skill contributed by team members and possible use of outside consultants	▪ Skill contributed by team members and possible use of outside consultants ▪ Supplemented easily from other functions within the company
Organization	▪ Functional group (e.g., Finance)	▪ Sponsor is focus on specific project ▪ Sponsorship varies from project to project	▪ Supervision is within functional area ▪ Culture is accepting but with need for tight control and validation	▪ Supervision is within functional area ▪ Culture is accepting but lesser need for tight control and validation
Management Process	▪ One-off reviews and decision making	▪ One-off reviews and decision making	▪ Decisions and actions are often focused on functional area ▪ Lack of system integration of decisions and actions	▪ Decisions and actions are focused on cross-functional impacts ▪ Highly developed sense of system integration of decisions and actions

Exhibit 4.2 Eight-Stage Process of Creating Major Change

Step	Action	New Behavior
1	Increase urgency	People start telling each other, "Let's go—we need to change things!"
2	Build the guiding team	A group powerful enough to guide a big change is formed and they start to work together well.
3	Get the vision right	The guiding team develops the right vision and strategy for the change effort.
4	Communicate for buy-in	People begin to buy into the change, and this shows in their behavior.
5	Empower action	Most people feel able to act, and do act, on the vision.
6	Create short-term wins	Momentum builds as people try to fulfill the vision, while fewer and fewer resist change.
7	Don't let up	People make wave after wave of changes until the vision is fulfilled.
8	Make change stick	New and winning behavior continues despite the pull of tradition, turnover of change leaders, and so forth.

Source: John P. Kotter and D. S. Cohen, The Heart of Change *(Boston: Harvard Business School Press, 2002).*

SELECTING A DESIRED TARGET STATE

Once the change management process is recognized and being applied, the guiding coalition team should size up an area to examine where improvement opportunities exist for predictive business analytics. Though major wins and successes are showcases, the path of concept proving will likely be a more desirable approach. Proof of concepts should be short term and have easily definable expected outcomes; require a reasonable level of resources, both people and tools; and strive for short-term wins that are tangible, impactful, and readily implementable.

The team needs to evaluate target-state alternatives, with each alternative evaluated based on decision criteria that achieve a best fit for launching the process. A tool used by many companies to review best-fit options is the quality functional deployment (QFD) approach. The value of QFD is that:

- The customer's wants and needs are inputs to this process.
- A matrix format is used to record vital information.

- Customer needs are translated into requirements.
- An analysis of requirements is facilitated and priorities are determined.
- The output is key to actions and issues for improving customer satisfaction based on customer inputs.

The QFD work involves a series of interrelated steps, as follows:

Step 1: Identify the customer wants and needs, often called the "whats."

Step 2: Customer ranking or weighting of customer needs:

- How important are the "whats" to the customer?
- Usually ranked on a 1 to 5 scale.

Step 3: How will we satisfy the customer needs ("whats")? What are the actionable items (process steps, inputs, etc.) to meet needs ("hows")?

Step 4: Understand the influence of each "how" on the "whats"—to what extent does each action correlate to the customer needs? Usually, a weighting is associated with each "what." For example, we could use a weighting scale of Strong = 9, Medium = 5 or 3, and Low = 1. These are wide enough to provide distinction in assigning weights. A caution: Often groups will try to put too fine a point on these weights and offer 8.5 instead of 9. This will make the evaluation process more difficult without adding much value.

Step 5: Identify the critical few "hows," multiply the "whats" weightings times the "how" relationship scores, and add together to obtain the total for the column.

A simple example (Exhibit 4.3) can best illustrate how QFD might be applied to delivering pizza. We have identified the "whats" and "hows" and assigned to each "what" an importance ranking. We then assign a rating to the "how" for each "what" and multiply the importance ranking times the requirements rating. For example, "Take order" is rated a 9 for "Ingredients are correct," and since this "what" has a ranking of 4 assigned to it, the total value of this "what" is 36 (i.e., 9 × 4). The next "what," "Pizza tastes good," is ranked a 5 in importance, but for taking the order it is only a 1 (least important) to satisfying this "what" or need. The total score is 41 (i.e., 36 + 5). By

Quality Function Deployment Matrix	Importance Ranking	Requirements (Hows)				
		Take order	Transfer order to kitchen	Prepare pizza	Bake pizza	Deliver
Customer Needs (Whats)						
Pizza is hot	5				9	9
Ingredients are correct	4	9	3	9		
Pizza tastes good	5	1		9	3	1
Low cost	2			3	1	3
Timely arrival	3		9	3	1	9
Relative importance		41	39	96	65	83

Exhibit 4.3 Importance Ranking

processing each of the cells, we can deduce that the best fit to satisfying the customer needs is finding a restaurant that prepares the best-tasting pizza with the correct ingredients and can deliver it hot.

Once priorities and capabilities are recognized, your organization needs to adopt a desired target state that is built on a solid analytical foundation. A suggested PBA continuous framework is discussed next and is depicted in Exhibit 4.4.

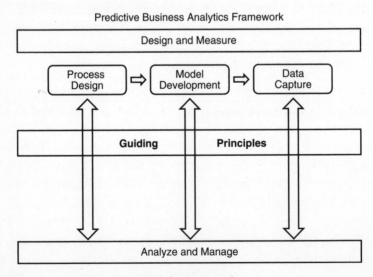

Exhibit 4.4 Predictive Business Analytics Framework

ADOPTING A PBA FRAMEWORK

As the opportunities for PBA become more important to the company based on early wins and success stories, it is now positioned to design and develop a process framework. An effective approach to developing and sustaining an integrated and continuous PBA process is best accomplished by deploying a framework that is continual (i.e., ongoing), coherent, and collaborative throughout the organization.

Exhibit 4.4 illustrates a framework that has been demonstrated to work effectively in numerous organizations. Although adaptations are always necessary, this framework can serve as a navigation or starting point to enable and encourage an organization to begin to build its capabilities and competences. It is important to recognize in setting up the analytical process that it should be organized to manage the whole value stream (i.e., all processes required to create value for the customer), rather than manage and optimize each process step in isolation.

DEVELOPING THE FRAMEWORK

For PBA to be effectively deployed by an organization, a continuous framework is essential to an effective understanding of the events, their relevant drivers, and their impact on decision making. The framework has two major components: (1) a structural element that focuses on design and measurement and (2) a managerial element that focuses on analysis and management.

In this chapter, we address the structural element, which is developed in three key steps:

Step 1: Process design.

Step 2: Model development.

Step 3: Data capture.

In Chapter 5, we address deploying the PBA function, which involves analyzing and reporting on the data and managing the process to take actions and make decisions.

Step 1: Process Design

The objective is to develop a process that enables the organization to predict a future outcome based on expected cause-and-effect relationships. The ability to leverage and/or refine historical relationships based on changes in current business conditions, competitive landscape, economic trends, and so forth is an inherent aspect of the process. But there needs to be caution about fundamental changes regarding the future that are not currently apparent. In essence, the ability to distinguish an anomaly from a fundamental change in cause-and-effect relationship is critical to implementing an effective process. It is important during process design to keep the guiding principles discussed in Chapter 3 continually in mind, and to test whether the new process highlights (1) a cause-and-effect relationship; (2) a balance of financial and nonfinancial, internal and external measures; (3) relevance, reliability, and timeliness; (4) integrity; (5) accessibility; and (6) the potential to drive desired behaviors.

The process design can be accomplished using a range of techniques, from highly quantitative mathematical models often used by investment banking organizations to drive their trading operations and trading decisions, to anecdotal approaches sometimes referred to as trial and error or experiential models (see discussion of Delphi method in the next subsection). Many organizations adopt a hybrid approach, and use regression analysis to form the baseline model. They then refine outcomes based on experience of senior managers and employees, who provide subject matter expertise due to their broad and deep experiences in the subject area. Although regression is more definable, is less subjective, and encourages collaborative involvement, managerial experience can help to foster ownership of the process among users within the organization.

In addition to determining the appropriate techniques, other factors that influence the process design are the resource requirements and organizational context. Resource considerations typically include defining the requisite analytical skills, functional knowledge and capabilities, and scope of decision authorities that need to operate to sustain the PBA approach. In terms of organizational context, the culture and the roles and responsibilities play a critical part in determining how best to deploy the process, and set the necessary boundaries around analysis and decision making. Understanding the cultural boundaries is critical to ensure that the PBA process assists in driving the right cultural incentives.

For example, a new product launch requires close coordination among several organizational functions, including marketing, sales, distribution, and manufacturing. The PBA process must (1) integrate the key drivers for each function, (2) reliably link cause and effect across the process, and (3) display alternatives for several key decisions and actions associated with the new product launch. Any one flaw in this chain of events could undermine the overall success of the product launch. In addition, the PBA process must demonstrate balance between internal (e.g., new product cycle time) and external (e.g., first-year sales) measures. Small to midsize organizations have an inherent advantage in that their size can facilitate more direct communications and interactions and better promote coordination of decisions and actions than is easily achieved in a large organization, where there can be a wide scope of responsibilities for decision making.

The decision as to which process design is better may be determined by a variety of considerations, including:

- **Industry dynamics** may affect an organization's business model and cycle (e.g., long cycle versus short cycle), competitive position, and regulatory and environmental boundaries.
- **Degree of impact** is another factor that influences the process design in terms of response time, cost impacts, order cycle, inventory levels, staffing levels, and capital investment.
- **Materiality and volatility** can also be key factors to consider in designing a workable process, especially by viewing the balance between these two factors. Exhibit 4.5 illustrates a set of managerial actions based on these factors, and appropriate actions arising from balancing these relationships in a way that would support the selected process design.

Step 2: Model Development

The initial step in model development is to determine the relevant relationship(s) between an input and its outcome. Inputs can be discrete events (e.g., change in London Interbank Offered Rate (LIBOR), new product launch); aggregated events (e.g., unemployment rates, consumer delinquencies); or structural events (e.g., new plant,

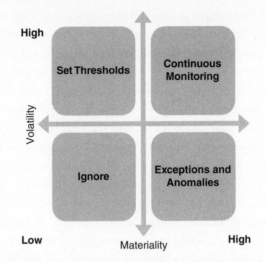

Exhibit 4.5 Suggested Actions in Relation to Materiality and Volatility of Data

regulatory approval). Often these inputs are referred to as "drivers," and can be viewed as leading indicators of future outcomes. Outcomes are the results of events, can be measured over a period of time, and can be viewed as lagging indicators. This is the basis of the "strong cause-and-effect" principle discuss in Chapter 3. For example, an airline makes reservations for a scheduled flight (input/aggregated event) and immediately can measure its change in passenger revenue (output/result). What is essential is to determine the likelihood that this relationship between events and outcomes has been consistent over time and that there is a reasonable expectation that these relationships will continue into future periods. There are numerous refinements to the airline example, such as pricing of reservations, cancellation policies, and historical trends (do airlines ever overbook?). After an organization understands and determines its drivers and results relationships, it can begin to develop, refine, and apply these relationships to its PBA process. A critical few driver relationships can account for a significant portion of the predictive results.

According to David Brooks, "If you asked me to describe the rising philosophy of the day, I'd say it is data-ism. We now have the ability to gather huge amounts of data."[4] Some even term this *big data*. This raises the question: What situations do quantifiable measurements hold forth as a mechanism to predict the future, and in which situations should we rely on intuition or gut feel to anticipate future events and outcomes?

Anyone who has ever watched a sports competition is familiar with expressions like "on fire," "in the zone," "on a roll," and "momentum." But what do these expressions really mean? In 1985 when Thomas Gilovich, Robert Vallone, and Amos Tversky studied this phenomenon for the first time, they defined it as follows: ". . . these phrases express a belief that the performance of a player during a particular period is significantly better than expected on the basis of the player's overall record."[5] Their conclusion was that what people tend to perceive as a "hot hand" is essentially a cognitive illusion caused by a misperception of random sequences. Gilovich, Vallone, and Tversky argued that time series results from basketball are indistinguishable from repeated uneven coin tosses (the coin might have a probability of success that is different from 50 percent).

Despite being extremely influential in the scientific community, their conclusions were highly controversial, as the vast majority of sports fans remained confident that sometimes players are indeed "on fire." Could it be the case that fans were right after all? The answer is a little complicated and depends on the specific task, but data seems to suggest that a hot hand does exist after all.

When studying this phenomenon, one major complicating factor is the presence of an opponent. The success probability of the task is no longer only dependent on the skills of the player, but is also confounded by the performance and strategy of the opposing player(s). A player who gets "in the zone" is likely to change the defensive strategy of the opposing team, making it more difficult for him or her to perform. Moreover, different opponents have different skills, leading to tasks of varying degrees of difficulty. All these factors make testing the existence of a hot hand very difficult, and require more complex models. These confounding factors can be overcome by considering tasks with minimal external interferences.

So how can one distinguish between a pure random series (essentially repeated coin tosses) and something else? This is where statistics comes in handy. Without delving deeply into the technicalities of the different statistical tests, we would like to just make note of a crucial point: The fact that a statistical test does not detect a phenomenon does not mean that this phenomenon does not exist. Most statistical tests are meant to reject a null hypothesis, and the fact that it cannot be rejected does not mean that the null hypothesis is correct. It might be the case that the statistical test used is not sensitive enough for the type of data and phenomenon being tested. It can also be the case that data is insufficient to yield a definite answer.

Interestingly, another contradicting example was shown in basketball three-point attempts, where it was shown that data actually present an "anti-hot hand." But, as mentioned before, in this framework the defensive strategy is important and is likely to influence the performance of the player—a player who has a "hot hand" will attract more attention from the defense, which can directly influence the results of future trials.

These examples basically show correlation between current results and previous ones, so an athlete's performance is not just repeated coin tosses. Does this mean that "success breeds success" and "failure breeds failure," or is there something else at hand?

Correlation and causation are often mixed together. From a statistical point of view, this is a difficult question. Human minds are often after reasoning and tend to misinterpret correlation as causation. To prove that something is actually causing something else, one has to perform more detailed studies and not rely on statistical correlation only. Correlation is essential for causation but not sufficient.[6]

Several techniques can be used to define and refine an organization's approach to model development or, more specifically, to driver identification and its related results. These techniques vary from quantitative methods to empirical methods. Several recognized methods or techniques are discussed next.

Regression Analysis

Regression analysis includes any techniques for modeling and analyzing several variables, when the focus is on the relationship between a dependent variable (i.e., outcome or result) and one or more independent variables (i.e., drivers). More specifically, regression analysis helps to understand how the typical value of the dependent variable changes when any one of the independent variables is varied, while the other independent variables are held fixed. In all cases, the estimated value is a function of the independent variables, and the variation of the dependent variable can be described by a probability distribution. For example, in the banking industry, the mortgage interest income (dependent variable) can be estimated based on the change in several independent variables, such as interest rates and employment rates. Regression analysis is not useful in all situations. For example, many cause-and-effect relationships are nonlinear, having two, three, or more related effects that are not captured by the analysis.

Nonlinear Systems

Nonlinear systems cannot be modeled as one-to-one, proportional relationships the way linear systems can. Rather, more complicated mathematical formulas that account for a greater number of variables are required to model nonlinear systems. As an example, if a company's sales perfectly predicted the price of that company's stock, the relationship would be linear. However, if the stock price is also influenced by market saturation, a decrease in available raw materials, and the introduction of new technologies by competing companies (e.g., commodity firms), the sales numbers alone may be insufficient to determine the value of the stock. Thus, sales figures alone cannot be used to linearly predict future stock price. Nonlinear systems use multiple variables to fit the data and do not fit the data with a straight line. The data may also be fitted through a series of successively better approximations as the equations used to describe the data are tweaked to better explain the overall pattern of that data. Nonlinear modeling is more complicated than simple linear or correlational modeling, and the skills needed to perform such modeling would be gained only with the required experience and expertise.

Monte Carlo Simulation

Monte Carlo simulation can help interpret the results of regression analysis. It is based on artificially re-creating a chance process over many occasions and observing the results.

Additionally, the impact of each independent variable can be measured and based on levels of confidence in the data. A series of scenarios can be developed and, based on managerial judgment and the data itself, used to effect operating decisions. For example, a consumer finance organization might seek to predict mortgage application fees and interest income, and establish a historical and statistically valid relationship with changes in interest rates, employment rates, and growth in national gross domestic product—that is, that the results were driven by these changes. Thus, when interest rates are lowered, employment rates increase, and there is growth in gross domestic product, it is then reasonable to expect increases in mortgage fee income and interest income over time.

Resource Capacity and Activity-Based Analysis

Resource capacity and activity-based analysis allows an organization to model how varying levels of resources (staff, working capital, and capacity) are being consumed through business processes to create end objectives such as a product or service. An organization needs to measure the effect its resource capacity and processes have on each other and how they contribute to overall profitability or service effectiveness. For example, a food distribution organization might consider an expansion of its business with a well-known food restaurant chain; this expansion of business would represent a significant increase in business volume of about 20 percent. The organization needs to understand the incremental impact the increased volume would have on the capacity of delivery, packaging, picking, and other warehousing resources and the expenses associated with the new business. They can determine the investments and operational changes necessary to meet the new level of demand. By analyzing the predictive nature of these process and activity relationships and their impact on consumed resources, the organization can negotiate higher prices and achieve higher margins that contribute to an over 20 percent improvement in profitability.

Delphi Method

The Delphi method is a systematic, interactive, nonquantitative technique for forecasting that relies on a panel of experts. The experts answer questionnaires in two or more rounds. After each round, a facilitator provides an anonymous summary of the experts' forecasts from the previous round, as well as the reasons provided for their judgments. Thus, experts are encouraged to revise their earlier answers in light of the replies of other members of their panel. It is believed that during this process the range of the answers will decrease and that the group will converge toward the "correct" answer. Finally, the process is stopped after a predefined stop criterion (e.g., number of rounds, achievement of consensus, or stability of results), and the mean or median scores of the final rounds determine the results. Digital communication has greatly facilitated the procedure.

One of the most important factors in Delphi forecasting is the selection of experts. The persons invited to participate must be knowledgeable about the issue and represent a variety of backgrounds. The number must not be too small to make the assessment too narrowly based, nor too large to be difficult to coordinate.

Experiential Insight

Experiential insight is a less structured form of the Delphi method. As a quick way to begin, operating managers often can select drivers based on operating experiences—but these need to be reliably correlated with results. Consequently, results should be tested against multiple variables using regression or statistical analysis. It is common to back-test these relationships, especially where these methods are based on experience and intuition. This is accomplished by applying actual historical data to these relationships, then measuring whether the cause-and-effect basis is within an acceptable margin of error given these known outcomes. After review, it is appropriate to adjust on an ongoing basis by looking for new drivers and/or by adjusting the weighting associated with each driver.

Scenario Analysis and Planning Scenarios

Scenario analysis and planning scenarios are a powerful tool in the strategist's armory. Certified Management Accountants (CMA) Canada's 2020 Vision paper, "Forecasting the Future Role of the Management Accountant" (www.cma-canada.org), identifies scenario planning as the defining organizational capability and a primary management accountant skill for the coming decade. Scenarios are particularly useful in developing strategies to navigate the kinds of extreme events we have recently seen in the world economy. Scenarios enable the strategist to steer a course between the false certainty of a single forecast and the confused paralysis that often strikes in troubled times. Scenarios have various features that make them particularly powerful tools for understanding uncertainty and developing strategy accordingly, including (1) expanding your thinking, (2) uncovering inevitable or near-inevitable futures, (3) protecting against groupthink, and (4) allowing people to challenge conventional wisdom. Scenarios typically cover various future states, one of which can include challenging events and conditions for the organization.

Step 3: Data Capture

Data capture for PBA differs in many ways from financial accounting. In financial accounting, recorded financial information is based mainly on historical transactions and judgments, whereas in predictive business analytics, information is often a blend of historical as well as forward-looking financial and nonfinancial data. Consequently, organizations can develop a series of estimates for their drivers and compile a set of possible scenarios. These scenarios can be weighted as to their likelihood of outcome by applying regression analysis (see previous discussion) and assigning a probability to each of the possible outcomes or actions.

In determining the better option for data capture, it is important to consider the context and relevance of how the predictive business analytics will be used, and the impact of actions being considered by management. Exhibit 4.6, an example from Southwest Airlines, illustrates these considerations. Revenues have high economic relevance and high variability, and thus would be updated daily; the predictive time horizon might be monthly. However, fuel prices, which also have high economic relevance and high variability, would be updated weekly, and the predictive time horizon might be three months. These are in contrast to those categories that have medium to low economic relevance and variability, and thus would not need to be tracked or updated as frequently.

	Economic Relevance	Variability	Operating Plan Response Speed	Update Frequency	Forecast Horizon
Revenues	High	High	High	Daily	Month
Labor Costs	High	Low	Medium	Semimonthly	Six Months
Fuel Prices	High	High	Medium	Weekly	Quarter
Maintenance Spending	High	Medium	High	Semimonthly	Six Months
Advertising Spending	Medium	Medium	High	Monthly	Year
Aircraft Rental Prices	Medium	Low	Low	Quarterly	Year
Landing Fees	Low	Low	Low	Annually	Year
Agency Commissions	Low	Low	High	Semiannually	Year

Exhibit 4.6 Predictive Business Analytics: Summary Matrix
Source: Steve Morlidge and Steve Player, Future Ready: How to Master Business Forecasting *(Hoboken, NJ: John Wiley & Sons, 2010). Courtesy of Southwest Airlines. Used with permission.*

For many organizations, data capture is complex. Often, the requisite data for a defined driver may not be readily available or easily accessible. Organizations can discover that, in the early stages of implementing predictive business analytics, the delivery of information is inefficient, cumbersome, or costly to capture. Such problems are especially evident when (1) systems are highly fragmented, (2) data definitions are inconsistent, (3) data capture is redundant and manually intensive, and (4) access is limited. A workable alternative is to identify surrogate drivers. These are drivers that, as the name implies, are used as substitutes for the more preferred but less available drivers. An organization will often begin to collect the preferred driver data for future availability.

As organizations mature, they should use more automated technology tools, not only to capture data but also to store and access large volumes of financial, nonfinancial, and operational data that can be effectively integrated in performing data analysis.

SUMMARY

In this chapter, the key elements of change management and meaningful organizational design of the PBA function have been described. Each element builds on the other, a form of mutual interdependence. The chapter further emphasizes the importance to determine the organization's capability maturity. We have witnessed in numerous organizations that a slow but steady maturing approach usually results in a sustainable and successful function. Management is more receptive to throwing its support to this function as it demonstrates its value contributions and improvements in meaningful and impactful decision making. The selection of methodology is often less important than the effectiveness of its outcomes and results. An extremely complex process may be more accurate, but if it is not understood by managers who use it, then it will likely not be as successful as a simpler but well-understood function.

NOTES

1. EPM Channel, March 2013.
2. John P. Kotter and D. S. Cohen, *The Heart of Change* (Boston: Harvard Business School Press, 2002).
3. John P. Kotter, *Leading Change* (Boston: Harvard Business School Press, 1996).
4. David Brooks, "The Philosophy of Data," *New York Times* op-ed column, February 4, 2013.
5. Brainstorm Private Consulting blog, 2012.
6. Charles Roxburgh, "The Use and Abuse of Scenarios," *McKinsey Quarterly*, November 2009, www.mckinseyquarterly.com/Strategy/Strategy_in_Practice/The_use_and_abuse_of_scenarios_2463.

CHAPTER 5

Deploying the Predictive Business Analytics Function

Corporate strategies are intellectually simple; their execution is not. The question is, can you execute? That's what differentiates one company from another.

—Larry Bossidy and Ram Charam, *Execution: The Discipline of Getting Things Done* (2002)

Flawlessly executing a well-designed predictive business analytics (PBA) capability is essential to improved decision making and management control. This requires a robust *integrated performance management program* that incorporates four critical elements:

1. **Adapting business strategy.** Responding to the changing business environment.

2. **Aligning performance management with strategy and operations.** Using the right resources for the right things and measuring the right indicators.

3. **Establishing dedicated analytical capabilities.** Pursuing fact-based, information-driven decision management practices to monitor and manage desired results.

4. **Conducting management operating reviews.** A disciplined and rigorous discussion among leadership team members of current and forecasted operating results and their implications to strategies and ongoing operations.[1]

In recent years, numerous studies have been conducted on business analytics. One such study highlighted that a significant number of companies fail to deploy credible analytical capabilities due to:

- Lack of understanding of how to use analytics to improve the business (38 percent).
- Lack of bandwidth due to competing priorities (34 percent).
- Lack of skills internally in the line of business (28 percent).[2]

In contrast, those organizations that deploy a focused and dedicated PBA capability, one that leverages well-designed performance measures, can achieve improved performance.

In one survey, 90 percent of respondents attained a positive return on investment (ROI) from their most successful deployment of predictive business analytics, and more than half from their *least* successful deployment.[3] In another survey, "Among respondents who have implemented predictive business analytics, 66% say it provides 'very high' or 'high' business value."[4]

> Ultimately, the goal of performance metrics is to drive improved results. Otherwise, why bother? Data show better performances among companies that employ performance metrics more frequently, and poorer performances for those that never or rarely leverage metrics to improve performance. For example, surveyed companies that reported their operating profit had grown by 15% or more in the past three years, more than 40% always leveraged metrics. In contrast, less than 10% said they never or not often leveraged performance metrics.[5]

Authors' note: Throughout the book we use measures and key performance indicators (KPIs) interchangeably, although some organizations have distinguished these terms. A working definition of key performance indicator (KPI) from Investopedia.com is: "A set of quantifiable measures that a company or industry uses to gauge or compare performance in terms of meeting their strategic and operational goals. KPIs vary between companies and industries, depending on their priorities or performance criteria. For example, if a software company's goal is to have the fastest growth in its industry, its main performance indicator may be the measure of revenue growth year-on-year. Also, KPIs will often be industry-wide standards, like 'same store sales' in the retail sector."

INTEGRATING PERFORMANCE MANAGEMENT WITH ANALYTICS

In today's business and economic environment, an organization must be adaptive to respond effectively to the magnitude and rapidity of change. Moreover, the complexities of an organization's business model increase the need for key management practices to be performed flawlessly.

Such essential practices include:

- Relentlessly communicating the strategy to the entire organization.
- Properly aligning process and organizational capabilities and resources with the business model.
- Visibly linking performance accountability and rewards (e.g., bonus, promotion) with operating results.
- Adapting strategies and operations to reflect evolving business realities.

Consequently, a critical element of an integrated PBA capability is the design and deployment of a meaningful and relevant *performance management system* that is aligned with both strategies and operations. Several necessary tools for achieving an effective capability and improved decision management are:

- A responsive performance measurement system.
- A management process that leverages information to drive decision making and performance accountabilities in concert with shareholder expectations.

- An allocation of sufficient resources, including access to critical and relevant data, availability and use of technologies, and assigned staff who possess requisite competencies and business acumen.
- An organizational design aligned to the business model that nurtures and rewards performance and manages risk taking.
- A sustainable strategic cost model.
- A well-crafted adoption of driver-based business planning and forecasting techniques and practices.

In this chapter, we delineate how performance measurement systems, robust management reviews by leadership teams, and organizational design and culture form the foundation for an effective PBA capability that contributes to improved and sustainable business results.

PERFORMANCE MANAGEMENT SYSTEM

A well-designed *performance management system,* as shown in Exhibit 5.1, enables a company to develop and utilize a coherent set of performance measures or key performance indicators (KPIs) that are translated into

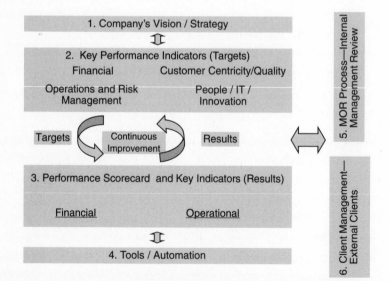

Exhibit 5.1 Performance Management Framework

concrete and operational terms that can be measured, communicated, and used to drive reporting, analysis, decision making, and action at both the business unit and individual levels.

Such performance management systems have delivered wide-reaching and varied benefits to organizations that use them. Companies that have taken the time to reappraise and redesign their performance scorecards have made themselves nimbler and more responsive to market shifts and more focused on what is important. The benefits of a good performance management system include:

- **Communication of strategy.** What we measure is the clearest way to define what we mean by the elements of strategy.
- **Alignment.** All teams and employees understand what they are responsible for, how it relates to the big picture, and how they fit into the organization.
- **Empowerment.** Once teams and employees are aligned and understand the way their work relates to others, they can make operating decisions much closer to the customer. This increases responsiveness and reduces the drain on management's time and attention.
- **Focus.** Tying performance measures to strategy and operating priorities helps separate the important from the nice-to-know and allows management to concentrate time and resources on the things that are critical for success.
- **Efficiency.** Well-designed performance measurement achieves focus and alignment with less effort. Sound process design and support tools allow the reporting to be less burdensome and timelier.
- **Execution.** What gets measured gets managed; driving the company to execute its strategy through operational excellence leads to growth and profits. Clearly, companies that get their performance measurement right can reap large rewards. If they can make decisions better and faster with more relevant information at their fingertips and present such information in a way that adds insight instead of overload, their ability to beat the competition grows. In fact, recent studies have shown that over the past three years, companies that manage by measures have

reaped returns almost twice as high as companies that manage by so-called common sense.

Performance scorecards are the core of an effective predictive business analytical capability by facilitating performance analysis, decisions, and resource allocations and providing feedback and commentary on comparative results. Exhibit 5.2 illustrates these elements with key business drivers providing the basis for structuring the performance scorecard, which are reflected in KPIs and performance reporting and drive performance analysis, decisions, and resource allocations. Continuous process improvements establish the basis for enabling better operating performances. Naturally, those benefits can be achieved only by creating a PBA capability within the organization consisting of individuals with diverse competencies, access to relevant and quality data, receptive management leadership team and operating groups of people, and a collaborative and results-driven culture.

Companies also have used a balanced scorecard (BSC) framework, as popularized by Robert S. Kaplan and David P. Norton,[6] as

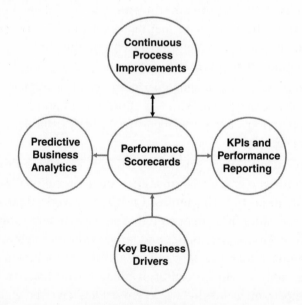

Exhibit 5.2 Performance Scorecards Serve as the Hub

an effective tool for developing a sound performance measurement system.[7] It helps to communicate the strategy to the organization and measures business performance aligned with strategic and operational performance targets and corresponding improvement initiatives.

An effective performance management system bridges the gaps among vision, strategy, and execution. It is a systematic framework to translate vision, mission, and strategy into a balanced and linked set of strategic objectives, operational initiatives, and performance targets for the entire company. *Performance scorecards* are typically organized into four perspectives, based on the premise that *financial performance* depends on *satisfying customers*, which results from having effective *business processes*, which in turn require necessary *organizational capabilities*, *competencies*, and *technology infrastructure*.

Sometimes companies will prepare a strategy map, which visually describes a company's overall business strategy and shows the cause-and-effect relationships among various elements required for executing on a strategy. It provides a clear, simple, and accurate representation of how these elements are integrated—and identifies the overlaps and gaps. Often, strategic themes are used as organizing principles linking strategic objectives and improvement initiatives. Examples of themes may include devoted customers, breakthrough innovation, and operational excellence. A strategy map also provides a framework to foster consensus, alignment, and commitment to the strategy by the leadership team and people across the organization.

IMPLEMENTING A PERFORMANCE SCORECARD

A performance scorecard system can be implemented in many different ways; however, a structured process encompassing three steps has been successfully implemented by many companies as part of their deployment of predictive business analytics. These steps are:

Step 1: Getting started.

Step 2: Defining key performance indicators/measures.

Step 3: Designing and developing predictive business analytics.

Step 1: Getting Started

In getting started to develop the PBA capability, an organization should consider several important factors. These are:

- **Executive sponsorship and culture.** Start with having an appropriate level of executive sponsorship and buy-in. In effect, management sets the tone for the organization from a "Why didn't we anticipate that event?" or "Who messed up?" to a more collegial and effective tone of "Okay, clearly things have changed. What are the major drivers of the change? What are the implications for our organization going forward? What actions should we be taking as a result?" Assigning organizational responsibilities and focus to this senior level ensures that the proper resources will be available and that behavioral actions and accountabilities will be recognized.

- **Governance and status updates.** Establishing guiding principles and a governance structure such as a steering committee to provide executive sponsorship is essential to success. It also provides a venue to highlight issues, concerns, and critical next steps.

- **Project management.** As with any new initiative, it is important to provide project oversight in terms of effective project management. This can be best accomplished when an implementation plan has been developed, and regular updates and status reports against this plan are provided to key stakeholders.

- **People.** The right mix of skills and competences will be needed among people assigned to properly analyze and communicate the insights and actions from the analysis. Such individuals should possess industry experience and functional expertise, and be able to exercise judgment that blends experiences with an acquired sense of practicality.

- **Tools.** Automated tools (e.g., spreadsheets, commercially available software) can facilitate the analytical process in sustaining the model structure, capturing and validating data, performing analytical routines, and reporting results.

- **Data standards.** Maintain a rigorous set of data standards that address the quality, integrity, and consistency of the captured data. It is appropriate for the organization to apply the same quality standards to this that are applied to financial accounting data and transactions. However, the data collection effort and cost of collection should not be burdensome and exceed the value of the data.

- **Process and work flow:** The organization should understand its value chain, core competencies, and their end-to-end operating process and supporting work flows. This enables the PBA capability to efficiently perform the analysis and to communicate its insights and selected actions and decisions.

- **Use of consulting services.** Organizations can turn to outside consulting services to design and implement this process, and/or supplement internal resources that may be lacking specific skills or expertise in critical areas. Regardless of how consultants are used, it is important that the organization ensures that the proper level of knowledge transfer is achieved, and that eventually the internal team assumes responsibility for performing and sustaining the process.

Step 2: Defining Key Performance Indicators/Measures

A performance scorecard builds upon strategy maps by identifying both financial and nonfinancial *measures* and *targets* to assess both strategic and operational performance. It balances short-term objectives with longer-term strategic goals, using both driver (i.e., leading) and result (lagging) measures. Many companies have multiple stand-alone improvement projects that are not prioritized, linked, or tied to business strategy. The performance scorecard requires management to evaluate and select those initiatives, such as customer surveys, reengineering, and other improvement projects, needed to achieve targeted performance levels and rates of improvement.

Exhibit 5.3 highlights differences between result and driver measures. In selecting measures, three important notions are:

1. Select a critical few.
2. Seek a balance between leading and lagging measures as well as financial and nonfinancial ones.

Exhibit 5.3 Types of Measures

Result (Lagging) Measures	Driver (Leading) Measures
Purpose ■ Focus on the performance results at the end of a time period or activity **Examples** ■ "Year-end sales" ■ "Market share" ■ "Cycle time" **Strengths** ■ Usually objective and easily Captured **Issues** ■ Result measures reflect success of past, *not* current, activities and decisions	**Purpose** ■ Measure intermediate processes and activities **Examples** ■ "Hours spent with customers" ■ "Number of mortgage applications" **Strengths** ■ More predictive in nature ■ Allows organizations to adjust behaviors for performance **Issues** ■ Based on hypotheses of cause and effect ■ Sometimes difficult to collect supporting data

3. Ensure alignment with strategies, operations, and organizational roles and responsibilities.

Selecting KPIs

The selection of KPIs is as much art as science. However, a few selection criteria may help in determining whether current KPIs are sufficient as predictive performance measures. Some hints are:

■ Gut feel measures are a good start—but are often not reliably correlated with results.

■ Results should be tested against multiple variables using statistical analysis and/or regression analysis.

■ Back-test results; that is, use past data to see if the measure would have predicted events.

■ Measure and adjust on an ongoing basis; look for new drivers.

A wonderfully revealing exercise can be conducted with various groups. Ask the group to suggest measures if they were general managers of a movie theater. Typically, the group suggests measures such as ticket sales, refreshment sales (often wanting to dive more deeply into specific measures such as popcorn vs. candy vs. soft drinks, etc.), employee attendance, and on-time starts. Now ask the same group to identify things that are important in selecting a theater for a hit movie that is showing in several nearby theaters. Do not be surprised that the group identifies things such as show times, parking, cleanliness, screen size, and sound systems. The point is that in selecting measures it is essential to select those measures from both an operating viewpoint and a customer viewpoint.

Exhibit 5.4 highlights another useful way to select measures by categorizing measures according to five groups. Each group provides an insight that may reflect an organization's business model and operating environment. For example, interest rates may be a strong predictor of revenues for a business that benefits from a low-interest environment (i.e., external/economic). Another may be programs that link capital spending for a company's updated web platform that embraces social media or adds self-service capabilities that generate revenues, reduce costs, or increase productivity. In each situation, there are measures that can be selected and used for predictive business analytics.

Two handy techniques we have found useful are *measures maps* and *measures templates*.

Measures Maps

Measures maps can be used to assess whether selected measures are the right critical few. This mapping technique is a visual way to demonstrate cause and effect, organizational alignment, accountability, and actionable information, which the PBA capability measures, analyzes, and reports to management.

For example, Exhibit 5.5 illustrates a measures map that describes a banking institution whose business objective is revenue (i.e., loan) growth. On the left side of the figure are organizational roles and responsibilities by management level (or function). The squares represent an aligned set of activities to achieve this objective with the circled items representing selected KPIs. As KPIs are captured and analyzed, this institution leverages these KPIs as predictive business measures. Thus, within this example, as the number of new leads increases and our close ratio remains constant, then our predictive model would indicate that our loan revenues would grow.

Conversely, if the number of new leads increases and our close ratio remains constant but our loan revenues decrease, then the PBA team would seek to obtain a deeper insight into the dynamics of this

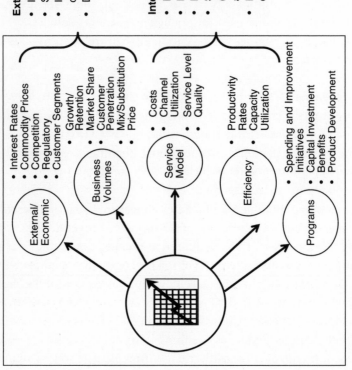

External Factors

- Identify potential causal drivers
- Statistically test historical relationships
- Identify vital few with strong correlation
- Develop and test predictive capabilities

Internal Factors

- Develop appropriate cost model
- Identify key drivers of cost
- Identify links to revenue model
- Separate scalable cost impacts (fixed and variable costs and activities)
- Identify links to productivity and capacity factors

External/Economic

- Interest Rates
- Commodity Prices
- Competition
- Regulatory
- Customer Segments

Business Volumes

- Growth/Retention
- Market Share
- Customer Penetration
- Mix/Substitution
- Price

Service Model

- Costs
- Channel Utilization
- Service Level
- Quality

Efficiency

- Productivity Rates
- Capacity Utilization

Programs

- Spending and Improvement Initiatives
- Capital Investment
- Benefits
- Product Development

Exhibit 5.4 Driver Framework

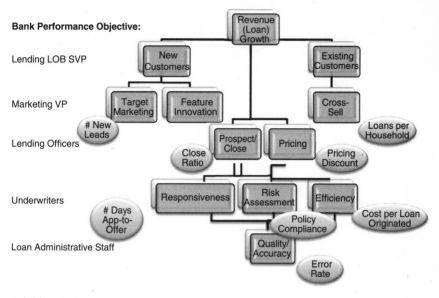

Exhibit 5.5 Measures Map

situation, often with the operating management who are responsible and accountable for these results. In this example, there may have been pricing discounts or a different mix of loans (e.g., size, type), or both. In any case, the team seeks to understand the dynamics of these factors, adjusts its revenue model, and likely begins to track relevant data to improve the KPI and subsequent predictive analysis and results.

Measures Templates

The other technique is measures templates (Exhibit 5.6) that support important aspects of defining and developing selected measures and their key elements, such as type, intent, frequency of update, formula definition, and data elements and sources.

Step 3: Designing and Developing Predictive Business Analytics

The analysis of results performed by organizations is the most crucial element of developing a meaningful PBA capability. In essence,

Exhibit 5.6 Measures Template

Key Performance Indicator: Names the KPI **Measure Type:** Lag (outcome) or Lead (driver) **Measure:** Names the measure **Measurement Intent:** Describes the measure and the reasoning behind its selection as an indicator of progress against this KPI	**Frequency of Update:** Identifies how often it is calculated **Units of Measure:** Identifies the units in which the measure will be reported

Measurement Definition/Formula: Provides a detailed formula for the calculation of a numerical value for the measure

Notes/Assumptions: • Clarifies terms in the formula as necessary • Highlights key assumptions underlying the formula	**Next Steps:** Describes the plan to overcome any deficiencies in getting the required data **Measure Period (for reporting):** Monthly Quarterly Yearly

Measurement Information Is: ___ Currently available ___ Available with minor changes	**Data Elements and Sources:** The data elements required to calculate this measure and the source systems, databases, documents, and so on of those data elements

Source for and Approach to Setting Targets: Identifies the report, document, system, or individual from which the information will be obtained

Target-Setting Responsibility: Person	**Accountability for Meeting Target:** Person	**Tracking/Reporting Responsibility:** Person	**Measure Availability:** Date **Target:** Date

Target	2012 Actual	2012 Projected	2011	2010
Lists numerical targets by year for the various components of the formula where relevant. For 2012 list targets by quarter and year.	1Q 2Q 3Q 4Q **Full Year**			

Source: © 2009 DecisionVu. All rights reserved.

predictive analytics' primary purpose is to identify "what we think the future will look like," and cultivate managerial decision making about operations and forward-looking actions that affect operating results and strategy execution.

Organizations may progress along a path of analytical maturity that reflects their capacity and capability to use predictive business analytics. The major stages are:

- Reactive.
- Systemic.
- Dynamic.
- Collaborative.

These stages can serve as a compass for organizations embarking on implementing a PBA capability. An organization that understands its current state is better positioned to progress to a desired future state by planning its series of activities, developing its model and drivers, allocating sufficient resources and people to the initiative, capturing relevant data, instituting necessary management review processes, and making key decisions needed to achieve its vision and improve operating performance and results.

A summary of these stages can help an organization to gauge its position and help to determine the extent of effort and resources to achieve its desired level of analytical capability:

- **Reactive.** At this stage, organizations' efforts are primarily focused on reacting to business events that often (1) are centered on departmental scope of responsibilities, functional activities, or performance measures, and (2) depend on a limited set of tools and techniques to pinpoint cause-and-effect relationships. This does not imply a lack of capacity to operate effectively, but more a sense of limited scope and narrowly defined set of corrective action alternatives.
- **Systemic.** At this stage, organizations' efforts are more broadly centered on cross-departmental focus on business events and some structural changes in products or markets. There are tools and techniques that are more battle tested and deliver a fair degree of insight into future operations or expected market results.

Also, during this stage there are clear signs of a systemic process, defined governance and risk management practices, and managerial discussions to guide decision making and corrective actions.

■ **Dynamic.** At this stage, organizations' efforts are more robust, with refined sets of driver and result/outcome relationships. Often, a dedicated group of business performance analysts/management accountants (1) routinely performs the periodic (monthly or quarterly) PBA program; (2) routinely captures key driver data; and (3) has a well-developed set of tools and management practices to discuss, decide, act upon, and monitor its decisions and corrective actions. Discussions are about current activities, threats, and opportunities, and the need to develop sustainable improvements rather than solve a problem or situation at a single point in time. Additionally, the level of confidence in credible forward-looking information used for decision making is fairly high, and more time is devoted to discussing the "What should we do?" and less about "Are the numbers right?"

■ **Collaborative.** At this stage, organizations' efforts are divisional and/or enterprise-wide and well developed. The ability to access key information is typically real-time (if needed) and is proactive in that trends and patterns are continuously captured and analyzed by business models and based on defined tolerances. Alerts and notifications can then be distributed to designated management and staff. There are clear accountabilities, and the interdependences of various departments or divisions are correlated to the business events and their anticipated consequences, thus rendering a more cohesive understanding of the organizational impacts. Managerial actions and intended results are continuously shared, and the organization's ability to learn and disseminate critical knowledge to other areas is advanced and trusted. There is clear buy-in of the process, and a strong sense of leadership and executive support for actions and improvements.

MANAGEMENT REVIEW PROCESS

The performance scorecard also enables a leadership team to manage performance proactively. The team learns continuously about its strategic and operational performance and thus understands where it needs to adapt strategy or correct marginal operating performance.

The performance scorecard explicitly identifies the critical drivers of success, which cut across an organization, and provides feedback on the execution of strategies as well as operating results. It fosters relevant discussion among the organization leaders regarding the key drivers of the business's success toward executing strategies. When used effectively, it becomes the leadership team's ongoing agenda that is reviewed and discussed on a dynamic basis for key decision making and managerial actions. Moreover, it is a powerful motivator of behavior and change; as such it can be used to appraise and reward performance.

> If you drop a feather and a rock at the same time from the same height, which will hit the ground first? At one point in history, this was a question for philosophers to resolve. Aristotle opined that the rock, because it was heavier, would fall faster and hit the ground first. Aristotle's armchair wisdom was not questioned until the 16th century, when Galileo, through cleverly designed experiments, proved him wrong and established an empirical basis for answering such questions about the physical world.
>
> Much the same way that an empirically based scientific method became the basis of our understanding of the world around us, analytics will eventually bring empiricism into business discourse and dethrone many of today's business practices.
>
> I chose this example to illustrate . . . how plausible yet armchair theories—like Aristotle's, lack any empirical evidence. (The falling hammer and feather experiment was actually performed by the crew of Apollo 15 on the surface of the moon, on August 2, 1971.) While highly specialized functions such as pricing or customer segmentation may be based on sophisticated models and empirical data, my contention is that the long-term impact of analytics will be in instilling a culture of data-driven decision making at all levels of an enterprise.
>
> A sophisticated and analytically oriented enterprise of the future will behave and operate differently from today's enterprise.[8]

Oftentimes, many organizations develop reporting tools to monitor the outcomes identified in their PBA process. Regardless of reporting tools and techniques, it is critical that a robust and structured management review process be sustained by the organization that reviews business results, assesses actions and key decisions, and links operational and strategic performance to their management process. For example, a global pharmaceuticals research and development organization developed a KPI system that reflected its strategic objectives of improving time, cost, and quality, and linked to the management leadership team's monthly review meetings. This integration of outcomes and management reviews contributes to effectively deploying PBA.

IMPLEMENTATION APPROACHES

Several alternative implementation approaches that should be considered are:

- **Pilot.** Often, organizations decide to implement these process changes by first selecting a pilot department or function. The benefit to this approach is that the investment and resources are small and manageable, the focus is narrow, implementation will be deployed within a reasonable time frame, and the effectiveness and long-term benefits can be gauged. Several considerations should be: (1) the receptiveness of senior managers to the pilot, (2) sufficient support from the leadership team, and (3) a clear recognition that this is a pilot and that its expectations of success are subordinate to its purpose to learn and refine the process, and to highlight ways to improve the process and the future use and extent of resources.

- **Scaled phase-in.** Scaled phase-in approaches are appropriate when an organization wants both to implement the process and to do so in a deliberate and steady manner without an inordinate commitment of resources to the process. This approach is similar to the pilot approach, but may involve several concurrent pilot departments or functions that offer the opportunity to (1) use broader sets of analytical focus and more extensive drivers, and (2) utilize the wider scope of management responsibilities and decision making.

- **Division-wide/enterprise-wide.** An organization will follow a pilot or scaled phase-in approach with a division-wide or enterprise-wide implementation. The focus could be on a division (e.g., consumer lending, retail banking, personal lines insurance) or a major department (e.g., education, public safety, graduate business school within a university). This approach has the additional benefit of truly understanding the scale and complexity involved in deploying the PBA process.

The choice of alternative implementation approaches is a matter of circumstances and priorities for an organization, and would be determined based on a realistic assessment of the alternatives, organizational resources, risks and consequences, as well as other key criteria that will influence a successful implementation.

Independent of implementation approach selected, an important set of steps would be back-testing and stress testing the predictive business analytical model. In the process of back-testing and stress testing, PBA models are developed with all data up to a fixed point in time being included. The model is then tested on its ability to predict how different types of transactions or events will fare given past known market conditions. In this manner, major events such as commodity shortages, competitor price changes, technological innovations, recessions, and the like can be assessed. If the model is able to accurately predict known events based on data leading up to those events, it is assumed that the model will correctly predict future events.

However, there is a trade-off between performance and fit. An over-fit model may accurately predict known events, but may not generalize to future events. In contrast, an under-fit model will not predict historical or modern events accurately. Finding this balance is a laborious process that requires a sophisticated understanding of how predictive models are constructed and of how modifications to these models will affect overall model performance. The models must be adjusted depending on the types of transactions being modeled and the types of events that are likely to influence market performance.

For example, predictive models that are based upon futures in such an area as commodities will be affected by weather patterns and the price of oil to transport these crops. Thus historical weather patterns and oil prices must be factored into the model and the model must be back-tested against historical changes in the price of oil and in the effects of extreme weather events, including hot or dry seasons that reduce crop yields. To develop effective, model-testing scenarios, the analytical team will need experience back-testing a wide range of models under many different market conditions. Furthermore, the team must have experience stress-testing these models to identify system stability and points of failure. In the context of predictive models, stress-testing includes increasing numbers of variables or conditions and different types of events to establish breaking points where the model no longer makes accurate predictions. Without knowing the limitations and properties of predictive models, one cannot determine the accuracy of the data being modeled. If the accuracy cannot be determined, the model is useless as an predictive tool. The team with experience back-testing and stress-testing its models will be able to consistently and reliably develop, test, and validate models capable of identifying and supporting the team's predictive business analytical capabilities.

CHANGE MANAGEMENT

A clear program for effecting change will help with the implementation of predictive analytics. There are many sources of information on effective change and project management. Each organization needs to ensure that it has the required technical and business competences to support and, where necessary, lead change management initiatives or arrange for the involvement of such capabilities. A change management role requires an understanding of the broader social and behavioral issues involved in implementing innovations and new ways of working. Several characteristics of effective implementation of a PBA capability are:

- **Communications.** Providing frequent and informative communications is essential to effectively introducing a PBA process capability to the organization. Generally, a communications plan can support a series of communication messages and activities. These can be conveyed with already established media vehicles, such as an organization newsletter, e-mail announcements, and success stories. What is important is that the organization is informed how the process contributes to operating results and tangible benefits.

- **Education.** Establishing a strong presence and understanding among managers and staff regarding why, what, and how the PBA capability can contribute to the success of the business. The use of peer sessions, one-on-ones with key players, and the designation of point person(s) are mechanisms to convey the narrative about why we are doing this, what we hope to accomplish, and how we are pursuing the end results.

- **Training.** Developing a series of training sessions is also an important step to ensuring the sustainable success of the PBA capability. These sessions might address technical methods and tools—for example, use of regression analysis, driver analysis, six sigma and lean, cause-and-effect analysis, and behavioral or managerial skills that facilitate interpersonal interactions and enhance collaboration.

SUMMARY

In this chapter, we have described many of the key structural components, such as designing a performance measurement system, selecting KPIs and drivers, and applying a management review process, that support a deployment of an effective predictive business analytics function.

Helpful templates and tools have also been shared to facilitate your journey to a more fact-based and data-driven capability to leverage predictive performance measures as a mechanism to achieve improved business results and a more competitive position in the marketplace.

We have emphasized that the PBA capability is more than just big data; it is a systematic and analytical process carried out by people with the skills and competencies to better understand those events and drivers that affect our business. In the end, it is about using selective information about our past to influence our future actions and decisions.

NOTES

1. Adapted from an article by Lawrence S. Maisel, "Fall Touchpoints," Forrester Research, Inc., October 2003.
2. "Analytics: The New Path to Value," IBM, 2010.
3. Predictive Analytics World survey: www.predictiveanalyticsworld.com/Predictive-Analytics-World-Survey-Report-Feb-2009.pdf.
4. Wayne Eckerson, "Predictive Analytics: Extending the Value of Your Data Warehousing Investment," TDWI Report.
5. Jill Jusko, Business Finance Online, October 19, 2011.
6. Robert S. Kaplan and David P. Norton, "The Balanced Scorecard: Measures That Drive Performance," *Harvard Business Review*, January–February 1992.
7. Lawrence S. Maisel is also one of the codevelopers of the balanced scorecard.
8. Kishore S. Swaminathan, "What the C-Suite Should Know about Analytics," *Accenture on the Edge*, February 2011.

Case Studies

CHAPTER 6

MetLife Case Study in Predictive Business Analytics

If you don't know where you're going, any road will take you there.

—George Harrison, "Any Road," from Lewis Carroll, *Alice In Wonderland*

M etLife is the largest life insurer in the United States by total assets. The industry is challenged by cost competition, fierce price pressures, and a low-interest environment.

At the peak of the 2008 financial crisis, MetLife opted to forgo Troubled Asset Relief Program funds and instead took advantage of a separate federal program to raise almost $400 million for general corporate purposes. The company also recapitalized with $2 billion of stock and more than $1 billion of debt. With all this excess capital in place, MetLife emerged from the financial crisis in relatively better financial health than many of its rivals and capitalized on this relative advantage when it acquired ALICO from

AIG in late 2010. The acquisition of ALICO is a positive
for the company's global strategy and entry into the Asian
marketplace and especially the Japanese market.

MetLife tries to set itself apart by pursuing corporate
customers in the mature U.S. markets. MetLife provides
life insurance for 90% of the companies in the Fortune
100. As the costs of life insurance policies represent a
largely immaterial part of the corporate budget, for these
companies price is not the only deciding factor. Corporate
customers look for a convenient and cost-effective way
to satisfy their benefit needs. MetLife's diverse product
portfolio allows its agents to bundle basic life insurance
with other ancillary benefits such as dental, accidental,
and health and create a tailor-made benefit suite. MetLife's
entrenched relationships have helped maintain a high
persistency rate.

Steve Kandarian was named CEO in May 2011. He
had been MetLife's chief investment officer since 2005. As
CIO, Kandarian was credited with strengthening MetLife's
investment portfolio. Sensing a brewing housing bubble,
he initiated a strategy to lower MetLife's exposure to
residential real estate by agreeing to sell the company's
holding of Stuyvesant Town in New York City for $5.4
billion in 2006.

Kandarian has been instrumental in steering the
company away from retail banking. Two months into his
CEO job, he announced that MetLife would seek to sell
its deposit banking business. In subsequent months, he
announced the sale of the residential mortgage lending
business, taking another step toward the goal of exiting
bank holding status. Under his leadership, MetLife has
been focusing its capital on expanding global insurance and
employee benefits businesses.

Strategically, management has announced its desire to
realign its operating divisions by geographic segments—the
Americas; Asia; and Europe, the Middle East, and Africa,
or EMEA. The new reporting structure should result in
a greater focus on international markets. In response to
this announcement, the company has initiated certain
changes, including the appointment of certain senior
executives in some of the key roles designed for the new
structure.[1]

Exhibit 6.1   MetLife Global Strategy

MetLife's current strategy is summarized in Exhibit 6.1.

One of those new executive appointments is the hiring of Martin Lippert as the new Executive Vice President and Head of Global Technology and Operations (GTO). GTO organizational structure spans critical technology functions, including infrastructure and architecture, enterprise and regional application development, vendor sourcing and real estate, and operations, including call centers and a group dedicated to enabling innovation. Each function is led by a business leader who is responsible for the respective function and is a member of the GTO leadership council (GTOC). Supporting Lippert is a chief of staff, led by Mona Moazzaz, and the newly created function within GTO, Global Business Efficiency and Effectiveness (BEE), led by Jeff Nachowitz.

In recognition of this new organizational structure and the imperative to manage on a global scale, Lippert introduced to MetLife a new program for performance management termed management operating review (MOR), which he has deployed with success at other global organizations. According to Lippert, "Managing the business starts with data." He further iterated the point: "Metrics are our business with leading indicators used to pinpoint performance and quality issues; these translate into the customer experience."

Consequently, the MOR program is a facts- and data-based management style that fosters a disciplined approach to performance management. It consists of key performance indicators (KPIs) that are aligned to MetLife's corporate strategies and detailed operating performance measures. KPIs (also referred to as metrics) entail core metrics (i.e., those common to all reporting units) and noncore metrics (those specific to a function or reporting unit). These metrics are organized by "books," which serve as the foundation for in-depth monthly reviews by Lippert, Moazzaz, Nachowitz, and GTOC direct reports who are accountable for their KPIs.

THE PERFORMANCE MANAGEMENT PROGRAM

The performance management program implemented for MetLife's GTO primarily consists of three key elements:

1. Performance management framework.
2. Key performance indicators reporting.
3. Management operating review (MOR).

Performance Management Framework

Exhibit 6.2 reflects the integrated performance management framework developed for the Global Technology and Operations organization. Its key characteristics are:

- Strategy is linked to operational outcomes and measures.
- Metrics are balanced between lead and lag and across multiple dimensions, including financial, customer, operating, risk, service quality, and so on.
- Key initiatives are used to foster results and facilitate improvements.
- Reporting and analysis provide feedback on where and how to improve.
- Management review sessions are focused on drivers and relative performance improvements.

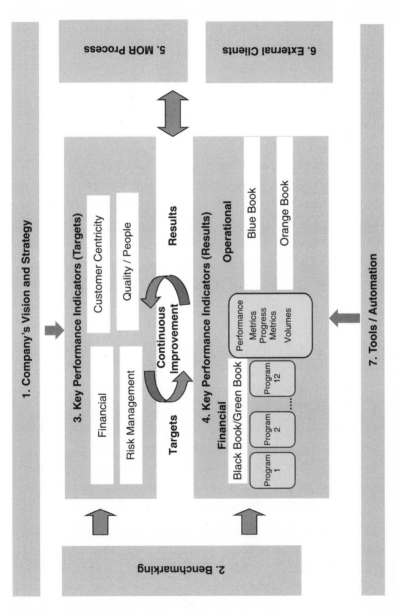

Exhibit 6.2   Performance Management Framework

89

- Information must be fact-based, actionable, and insightful to drive quality decision making.
- Rewards are used to influence desired behaviors, enforce organizational alignment and cultures, and ensure coherent decision making.

Key Performance Indicators Reporting

Within this performance management framework resides a series of interrelated sets of KPIs that are defined, reported upon, and organized within set of four books. Lippert favors this data-driven approach but also states that "High-level indicators do not remove responsibility to manage the detail; otherwise, you lose perspective on how well you are managing."

These books provide a management structure for Global Technology and Operations by:

- Creating consistent and transparent reporting.
- Leveraging comparative information to identify areas of opportunity and potential risks.
- Establishing targeted results that are aligned with strategic plans and based on relevant industry and operating benchmarks.
- Fostering cohesion with internal business partners and external clients (i.e., customer centricity).
- Producing a performance scorecard to drive performance analytics, decisions, and resource allocations.
- Facilitating management discussions among direct reporting units to highlight current and forecasted operating results and ongoing improvement actions.

From the perspective of David Sullivan, assistant vice president within BEE, "The books establish a standard foundation for the various types of functions that fall within GTO and facilitate the management reviews each month with data captured as key performance indicators. Giving each book a color ties the information together into a unified process and helps the organization understand what is critical to senior management."

Each book's objectives are:

Green Book Objectives

- Provide sustained focus, including program oversight, on priority GTO optimization activities, of which cost savings is just one of the many outputs rather than the singular goal (continuous improvement, process reengineering, etc.).
- Develop and track both financial and nonfinancial measurements of success and transformation.
- Provide a framework that assigns functional accountability for savings initiatives while allowing for savings impact across the organization.

Black Book Objectives

- Provide standardized monthly financial reporting templates.
- Promote transparency and accountability.
- Provide early warning for corrective actions.
- Financials serve as reference throughout the month for inquiries and Executive Summaries and are used for monthly reviews and preparation of the quarterly Dedicated Business Review (DBR), a recurring working session of senior corporate executives.

Blue Book Objectives

- Establish a working set of management metrics (e.g., volumes, customer experiences/service quality, talent).
- Create an ongoing metrics-based dialogue about the organization's performance up and down the management chain.
- Leverage facts to understand trends, establish objectives, and track progress.
- Facilitate internal and external benchmarking.

Orange Book Objectives

- Standardize reporting of key GTO programs.
- Provide key programs' status and associated metrics—on schedule, on budget.

- Standardize reporting of program performance metrics (e.g., risk indicators).
- Enable GTOC governance review against financial, execution, and business risk.
- Create early warning framework for critical management issues.

Management Operating Review

The monthly operating reviews are focused on explaining the implications of the data collected through these sets of books: Is the organization on track? What help do we need? Can we overachieve? What trends are we seeing? According to Lippert, "The MOR needs to be relevant to staff and clarify to them 'How do I fit in?'"

Information is reported as actual results and forecasts. Each responsible executive has selected those KPIs that are critical to the respective unit's success and has identified key drivers (i.e., predictive business measures). For example, within GTO there is a unit that focuses on innovation. This group's goal is to facilitate innovation ideas among employees that will translate into dollar savings or added revenues. The group routinely measures the number of ideas generated, those selected as feasible, and those implemented, including measuring amounts of savings or increased revenues, executing customer centricity, and enabling employee engagement. In this way, the group has the ability to predict the flow of new ideas yielding monetary and nonmonetary benefits. This is one of the ways to deploy MetLife's predictive business analytics capabilities.

Benchmarking

The organization will determine and, where available, utilize the relevant set of internal and external benchmarks, and will leverage the set of books to standardize internal views, trends, comparisons to competitors, and external benchmarks, where available and comparable.

A summary of MOR content is given in Exhibit 6.3.

Exhibit 6.3 Management Operating Review Content

I. Executive Summary	II. Financials (Black Book)
▓ Follow-ups from prior MOR Highlights	▓ Month/Quarter/YTD vs. Forecast/Plan
▓ Finance	▓ Full Year vs. Forecast/Plan/Prior Year
▓ Audit and Risk	▓ Six-Month Trend (Three Months Actual, Three
▓ Productivity/Expense Management	Months Forecast)
▓ Strategic Project Status	▓ Eight Quarter Roll Forward
▓ Achievements	▓ Opportunities/(Risks) vs. Forecast
▓ Key Issues	
▓ People	
III. Productivity Portfolios (Green Book)	**IV. Key Initiative Status Report** (Orange Book)
▓ Infrastructure	▓ Top Programs
▓ Enterprise App Development	▓ KISR (Key Initiative Status Report)
▓ Regional App Development	
▓ Corporate Real Estate	
▓ Procurement	
▓ Global Operations	
V. Performance (Blue Book)	**VI. Appendix**
Management Metrics:	▓ Topical Subjects
▓ Core metrics	▓ Supporting Documentation as Needed
▓ Innovation	
▓ Operations	
▓ Procurement	
▓ Real Estate	
▓ Technology—Infrastructure and App Development	

IMPLEMENTING THE MOR PROGRAM

With this as a backdrop, Nachowitz's BEE team engaged DecisionVu, management consultants, who specialize in designing and developing performance management programs, to assist them to complete a project to structure and implement its MOR program. The program used predictive business analytics as a critical foundation for its success and performed a series of interrelated steps:

Step 1: Establish policy and charter for a MOR program.

Step 2: Develop KPIs/measures.

Step 3: Establish data management.

Step 4: Develop reporting tools and processes.

Step 5: Conduct management reviews.

Step 6: Build organization and supporting resources.

Step 7: Maintain communications and change management.

Step 1: Establish Policy and Charter for a MOR Program

A. Establishing the Mandate for the MOR Process and Management Metrics

The Global Technology and Operations Committee (GTOC) consisting of all senior executives within the GTO organization has established as part of its business objectives that within and across GTO organizations a set of management metrics and a MOR process be establish to manage and achieve targeted operating results and ensure strategic performance.

B. Important Principles about the MOR Process and Management Metrics

- Effective measures will drive the right (desired) behaviors—poorly defined measures can result in unintended and unforeseen behaviors, actions, and decisions.
- An optimal set of metrics is not gotten the first time around; it is an iterative process.
- It takes a while for people to understand and perceive the benefit of performance management—particularly the degree of alignment and focus on results that occurs.
- It's a journey, and it's important that leadership stands firm when it is tested as to whether leaders will stick with the process.

C. Selecting Management Metrics

Representatives from each GTO organization have developed and concurred on a set of business-specific management metrics and a set of core metrics. Each GTO organization will define those measures that are applicable to its business activities. Each performance measure may differ in specific usage but will represent a means to measure the performance of the specific GTO organization.

For example, total information technology (IT) spend as a percentage to invest in/run the business is a business-specific management metric. Each business unit (BU) should define those specific components of the measure to best reflect its development and business activities. Often a metrics catalog is developed as a means to document the metrics and to provide a handy reference source for staff who are not familiar with the specific metrics. The catalog highlights important aspects of defining and developing selected measures and their key elements, such as type, intent, frequency of update, formula definition, and data elements and sources. (See Exhibit 6.4.)

Certain core metrics have been established for each GTO organization function. Each GTO organization will report its results of these core metrics. For example, involuntary turnover is a core metric with each GTO organization reporting its results and accompanying commentaries.

D. Revising/Adapting Management Metrics

Each GTO organization may elect to revise or adapt its initial management metrics, depending on circumstances reflective of its business activities. Such changes should be completed in conjunction with the budget and goal setting cycles for the GTO organization and should follow governance practices for developing measures by completing a measures template, review, and approval by the GTO organization, and updating reporting tools. RACI charts were developed to document these governance policies and practices (see Exhibit 6.5).

A responsibility assignment matrix, also known as a RACI matrix (pronounced /ˈreɪsiː/) or linear responsibility chart, describes the participation by various roles in completing tasks or deliverables for a project or business process. It is especially useful in clarifying roles and responsibilities in cross-functional/departmental projects and processes. RACI is an acronym that was derived from the four key responsibilities most typically used: *responsible, accountable/approval, consulted,* and *informed.*

E. Organization and Communications

The BEE team conducted a series of meetings with each of the senior leaders to communicate the objectives of the MOR program, describe

Exhibit 6.4 Metrics Catalog

Metric Name	Metric Operational Definition	Metric Intent	Metric Formula	Availability	Scope	Confidence
IT infrastructure spend % to invest in/run the business	**Run the business**—Expenses required to sustain existing IT functionality from an infrastructure perspective. **Grow/invest the business**—Creating new value or capability by responding to new or changing technologies	To determine the efficiency of the organization	Total discretionary (invest/grow the business) spend divided by the total nondiscretionary spend and ISLA services (run the business)	Yes	U.S.	High
AIX utilization %, total #, # virtualized	**AIX utilization %**—Amount of server resources used. **Total #**—Number of operating system images, includes all platforms, all environments. **# Virtualized**—Number of operating system images running in a virtual environment	**AIX utilization %**—General use of data center resources. **Total #**—Amount of data center resources made up of AIX/POWER hardware. **# Virtualized**—Adoption of virtualization technology	**AIX utilization %**—90th percentile of CPU resources used divided by the amount of CPU resources allocated from active resources. **Total #**—the number of operating system images; includes only AIX servers, all environments. **# Virtualized**—The number of operating system images running in a virtual environment.	Yes	U.S.	High
Wintel utilization %, total #, # virtualized	**Wintel utilization %**—Amount of server used. **Total #**—Number of operating system images. **# Virtualized**—Number of operating system images running in a virtual environment.	**Wintel utilization %**—General use of data center resources. **Total #**—amount of data center resources made up of x86 hardware. **# Virtualized**—Adoption of virtualization technology	**Wintel utilization %**—90th percentile of CPU resources used divided by the amount of CPU resources allocated from active resources. **Total #**—the number of operating system images; includes x86 stand-alone and virtual platforms, all environments. **# Virtualized**—The number of operating system images running in a virtual environment	Yes	U.S.	High
Mainframe utilization %	Amount of mainframe computer resources used	General use of mainframe resources. Due to batch components of mainframe, the peak and 90th percentile utilization are expected to remain stable and are not indicative of capacity requirements.	90th percentile of used resources divided by the amount of available MIPS (Note—specify calculate at peak times)	Yes	U.S.	High

Exhibit 6.5 Governance Matrix

Sub Process	Decisions/Actions	Governance Model				
		EVP & Head of GTO	GTO Planning & Effectiveness	GTOC Member	GTO Business Partner	Point Person
Define Management Metrics	Define management metrics		C	R		—
	Complete measure template (Exhibit A)			A		R
	Submit to GTO P&E team		A			R
Define Production Schedule	Establish dates and responsibilities		R/A			—
	Define follow-up procedures/work flows		R/A		—	—
	Define escalation policies and procedures		R/A		—	—
Define Data Source Systems	Identify source system owner		C	A		R
	Modify source system data		A	A		R
	Modify source system data calculations			C		R
Define Security Privileges	Authorize users		A	R		—
	Define scope of authority (e.g., region/country)		A	R		—
	Designate level of security (read, add, change, delete)		A	R		—
Process Data Collection	Define data collection template		R/A			C
	Approve rules for validating source files		A	R		C
	Approve rules for validating reported values		A	R		C
	Define override approval process		A	R		C
	Define default values for override		A	R		C
	Designate positions authorized to approve override values		A	R		
	Define process to correct overrides		R/A			
Submit Data Collection	Prepare data collection template					R

(continued)

97

Exhibit 6.5   (continued)

Sub Process	Decisions/Actions	Governance Model				
		EVP & Head of GTO	GTO Planning & Effectiveness	GTOC Member	GTO Business Partner	Point Person
	Validate data and metric calculations			A		R
	Review metric results			A		R
	Develop talk points			A		R
	Review talk points			A		—
	Submit data collection template		A	A		R
	Request deadline extension for submission			A		R
	Follow up on delayed submission			R		—
Review Data Collection	Review metric results		R/A			
	Highlight data errors		R/A			
	Request corrections		R/A			
Upload Data Collection	Upload data collection template		A			R
	Reconcile to control totals			R		R
	Post prior period adjustment					
Distribute Reports	Approval to run MOR reports (Blue Book)		A			
	Distribute reports		R/A			
Conduct MOR Meeting	Capture follow-up actions		R	A		R
	Track and report progress					

its mechanism and timetables, and request that a point person be designated for the business unit. The point person role was summarized as follows:

- Introduction: Monthly, each GTO departmental point person is to provide talking points for each metric. The objective of the talking points is to elaborate on the metric, add business context, and answer standard questions.
- Interpretation comments (required):
  - Performance versus plan/forecast.
  - Explanation of target and performance trends.
  - Actions intended to improve performance.
  - Any changes in metric definition/regional coverage.
  - Any additional information that would be useful to provide a clearer understanding of the business and/or financial impact of the metric.

F. Defining Reporting Structure

Next, a reporting structure needed to be established that would allow operating executives and their teams to define and maintain their own sets of KPIs and other operational reporting metrics while still meeting the objectives of MOR and BEE requirements.

After a series of discussions with key operating leads and their reporting staff (point persons), the team devised a recommended structure, depicted in Exhibit 6.6.

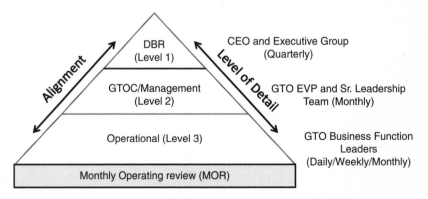

Exhibit 6.6 Reporting Structure

The recommended reporting structure in Exhibit 6.6 is:

- Level 1: Enterprise-level metrics (i.e., Dedicated Business Review).
- Level 2: GTOC MOR management metrics.
  - Core metrics (provided by human resources, finance, audit, etc.).
  - Metrics specific to each organization.
- Level 3: Operational metrics.

"A key performance indicator is one selected because it measures or reports on something in the organization closely connected to its ability to realize its goals and strategy."[2]

Step 2: Develop KPIs/Measures

A. Guiding Principles

The BEE team defined a set of guiding principles that would be the basis for selected KPIs. These were given the acronym SMART, which reflected the following characteristics:

Simple—The metric should be easy to understand and indicative of performance. Does it have a clear definition? Can it be generated without complex calculations?

Measurable—Is it easy to measure? Is the required data readily available? Is the metric specific and calculated consistently? Can it be benchmarked?

Achievable—Is the metric achievable? Can the team responsible for it influence it? Do we understand the drivers behind it?

Results oriented—Does the metric focus on measured outcomes and actions? Are these relevant to the business as a whole? Does the metric align with intended business purposes and intended strategies?

Timely—The metric should be relevant and reported within a reasonable time frame.

B. Defining Management Metrics Specifics and Calculations

A management metrics template (see Exhibit 5.6 in Chapter 5) was used to assist each GTO organization to define and document its management metrics as well as to facilitate a comprehensive capture of necessary information needed to sustain the reporting and analysis of management metrics.

Each template required that the method for calculating a management metric be specified along with defining the included data elements, the data source system, and the algorithm for calculating the measure as well as other important information.

GTOC has defined a set of core metrics (e.g., human resources, finance, audit), which are reported by GTO organizations and summarized for the entire GTO enterprise.

C. Obtaining GTO Organization Final Review and Approval

Each GTOC member develops individual targets to measure the performance of its GTO function. It is necessary that each GTOC member reviews and assesses how well management metrics are aligned and, to the extent appropriate, recommends changes (i.e., additions, revisions, or deletions) to those measures. A final set of management metrics was presented to the GTO organization leadership team for their review and approval prior to submitting to BEE for final approval.

D. Book Reporting

Each GTO organization is responsible for capturing, validating, and reporting the results of its management metrics on a periodic basis. Reports that incorporate aggregated information are not routinely distributed, although individual GTO organization reports with comparative results are occasionally distributed among GTO organizations for discussion and sharing of better practices. These usually are regional comparisons and core metrics such as employee turnover. According to Doug Bridges, a director in BEE, "The regular process of creating the books and holding a monthly operating review creates visibility into the departments and transparency across regions. This is an essential discipline to give senior management the information to run a global business."

The reporting of KPIs with monthly actual and target results provides management with a clearer understanding of ongoing performance results and can be accompanied by narratives and discussions on future actions and decisions. Exhibit 6.7 illustrates for MetLife one of these reported metrics.

IT Invest % — illustration

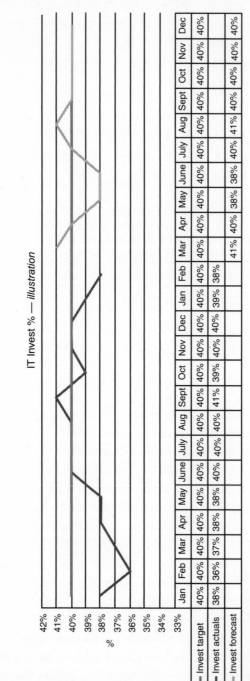

	Jan	Feb	Mar	Apr	May	June	July	Aug	Sept	Oct	Nov	Dec	Jan	Feb	Mar	Apr	May	June	July	Aug	Sept	Oct	Nov	Dec
Invest target	40%	40%	40%	40%	40%	40%	40%	40%	40%	40%	40%	40%	40%	40%	40%	40%	40%	40%	40%	40%	40%	40%	40%	40%
Invest actuals	38%	36%	37%	38%	38%	40%	40%	40%	41%	39%	40%	40%	39%	38%										
Invest forecast															41%	40%	38%	38%	40%	41%	40%	40%	40%	40%

Exhibit 6.7 Illustrative KPI

E. Forecasts and Targets

Each BU is responsible for assigning relative weights to each management metric for the purpose of determining relative importance and priority setting among measures within the BU. Additionally, each BU will establish a target value that can be used to compare to actual performance, third-party benchmarks (when available), and longer-term goal setting. These forecasted results and comparisons to targeted values are valuable as predictive analytical tools that can be used by managers to adopt alternative actions, reallocate resources, revise decisions, and so forth.

Step 3: Establish Data Management

A. Information Flow

Data sources are defined and captured, validated, errors corrected, and so forth, and operating processes are established to provide reporting of management metrics. Exhibit 6.8 summarizes the MOR process's information flow.

B. Production Calendars and Closing Process

A production calendar is documented and serves as a means to establish a routine closing process each month. The production calendar highlights the sequence and describes key steps in the monthly close process, assigned responsibilities, and dates when data is due.

Exhibit 6.9 illustrates a MOR monthly production calendar.

Step 4: Develop Reporting Tools and Processes

A management metrics reporting system has been developed as the preferred tool to capture and report management metrics results and commentaries.

- Each GTO organization can define and produce its own dashboards and management reports (i.e., leveraging reporting formats), as well as determine its reporting relationships.
- Each GTO organization can define the reporting frequency (e.g., monthly, quarterly) for dashboards and management reports.

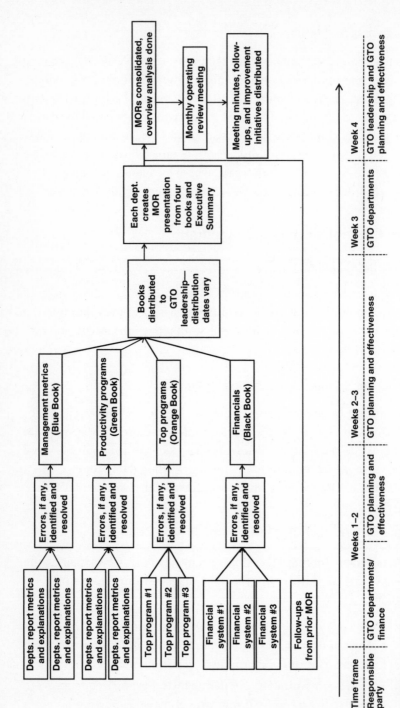

Exhibit 6.8 MOR Process—Information Flow

Time frame		Weeks 1–2	Weeks 2–3	Week 3	Week 4
Responsible party	GTO departments/ finance	GTO planning and effectiveness	GTO planning and effectiveness	GTO departments	GTO leadership and GTO planning and effectiveness

Step	Description	Responsibility	Timing
1. Initial Data Collection	Individual metric data is captured at the source.	Point person	Prior to BD 8
2. Initial Data Validation	Data is validated.	Point person	Prior to BD 8
3. Prepare Template	Template that will be sent to GTO is prepared.	Point person	Prior to BD 8
4. Talking Points	Talking points are added to the template.	Point person	Prior to BD 8
5. Data Collection Template Sent	Templates are provided to GTO.	Point person	BD 8
6. Data Validation	Data is validated versus prior submissions.	GTO effectiveness	BD 9
7. Analysis	Data and talking points are analyzed.	GTO effectiveness	BD 9
8. Questions	Questions are provided back to point person.	GTO effectiveness	BD 9
9. Answers	Answers to questions are provided back to GTO.	Point person	BD 11
10. Produce Blue Book	Blue Book is run and produced.	GTO effectiveness	BD 13

Exhibit 6.9 MOR Monthly Production Calendar

■ Training and other operating support should be coordinated through the BEE support team.

Step 5: Conduct Management Reviews

Each GTOC member should establish a defined and consistent management review process (ownership, accountabilities, etc.) for the organization's management and operating metrics. These reviews should leverage the use of measure owners and encourage the management resources of the entire leadership team.

Step 6: Build Organization and Supporting Resources

A. Organizational Roles

Each BU will be responsible for assigning an individual (i.e., point person) to fulfill organizational roles necessary to sustain the management metrics and MOR process. The point person's roles and responsibilities are:

■ Identify source(s) of metric.
■ Identify resources (our team will communicate with the point person).
■ Collect and validate data.
■ Upload data.
■ Remediate data at the source.
■ Streamline and improve collection process.
■ Prepare analysis and talking points.
■ Conduct ongoing maintenance.
■ Ensure standardization across regions and business units.

B. BEE Support Team

The BEE support team is responsible for:

■ Ensuring consistency and comparability.
■ Promoting communications.
■ Leveraging cross-functional implementation efforts and investments.

- Facilitating designated GTO functions by providing guidance in metrics selection, report production, and development of key business operating summaries and explanations.
- Integrating management metrics with other reporting books and processes such as DBR.
- Administering metrics catalog in accordance with governance practices.

C. Share Point Site

BEE has set up a share point site to support the monthly operating review process. The site includes all four management books (Black, Blue, Green, and Orange); monthly MOR presentations; the current monthly production calendars; and other support materials. Access is currently set up for GTOC members, their designated point people, and a limited number of other key associates.

The share point site is organized among folders as follows:

- **MOR.** Management books for each color and prior periods that include historical information and narratives as well as agreed follow-up actions and decisions.
- **Practice guide.** Describes the practices for defining and implementing management metrics.
- **Exhibits.** Exhibits of management metrics as well as illustrative examples of process flows, forms and templates, and so on are available for review.
- **Training materials.** These will be added as they are developed in the future.

Step 7: Maintain Communications and Change Management

- A network of point person coordinators has been organized as a means to promote and facilitate ongoing communications and to conduct periodic discussions regarding the activities needed to maintain and enhance the KPI system and MOR program.
- The point person network should promote cross-GTO organization best practice sharing and establish a medium for open discussion and problem resolution.

BENEFITS AND LESSONS LEARNED

Ultimately, the goal of performance metrics is to drive improved results. Otherwise, why bother? Data show better performances among companies that employ performance metrics more frequently, and poorer performances among manufacturers who never or rarely leverage metrics to improve performance. For example, of manufacturers who reported that their operating profit had grown by 15% or more in the past three years, more than 40% always leveraged metrics. In contrast, less than 10% said they never or not often leveraged performance metrics.[3]

According to Jeff Nachowitz, BEE's Vice President: "The insurance industry has become very competitive, exacerbated by a long-term low-interest-rate environment. As such, small errors in technology and operations can result in significant risk. Staying ahead in a fast moving market requires creating a forward-looking management process that provides early warning into potential issues as well as highlighting areas of opportunity. Making fact-based decisions in a dynamic environment increases the odds of making the right decisions."

SUMMARY

This chapter describes how MetLife established its process to improve operating performance by developing a performance scorecard framework and reporting process. This process, termed MOR, is one that integrates fact-based key performance indicators into its management reporting and review. This provides the foundation for MetLife's leadership team and its Global Business Efficiency and Effectiveness group to develop and utilize KPIs for managing with predictive business analytics to foster better and faster decision making and adapted operational practices.

NOTES

1. Excerpted from Morningstar Analyst Note dated January 30, 2013, "MetLife Is Close to a Banking Exit," by Vincent Lui, CFA.
2. Ventana Research, "Choosing the Right Performance Management Metrics," 2011.
3. Jill Jusko, Business Finance Online, October 19, 2011.

CHAPTER **7**

Predictive Performance Analytics in the Biopharmaceutical Industry

There are two possible outcomes: if the result confirms the hypothesis, then you've made a measurement. If the result is contrary to the hypothesis, then you've made a discovery.

—Enrico Fermi

Chapter 7's author, Eileen Morrissey, is the president and founder of Medicines Differentiation Analytics, LLC (www.medifvu.com), following more than a decade of leadership positions in large biopharmaceutical companies (including Merck and Pfizer). Her company provides analytic differentiation valuation analysis to biopharma medicine teams, licensing support to international universities, and performance management consulting. She has a patent pending on her intellectual property, MedifVu. Ms. Morrissey is a CPA and lean six sigma black belt.

109

For decades, 80 percent margins in the biopharmaceutical industry made up for a lot of mistakes. More recently, due to increased domestic and global competition, stronger government price controls, new health care regulations, and the increasing power of the payer/insurance companies, the days of healthy biopharmaceutical margins are over. Today, all small and large biopharmaceutical companies are struggling to find new ways to discover, develop, commercialize, manufacture, and distribute medicines more efficiently and effectively. For many, this journey has been a tough struggle. For some, they have been very successful in certain areas of the business and are rising above the rest. In this chapter, we explore a few of those success stories and describe the efforts that have led to their successes.

The pressures to do more with less have forced biopharmaceutical companies, like other industries, to look at how their traditional performance metrics were rewarding functional/siloed excellence at the detriment of company-wide excellence, or encouraging innovation or lower costs at the detriment of speed to market. In addition, the ability to use predictive business analytics and related performance measures (either in financial results or in market success of a new drug) has become increasingly important to this industry.

Most of the large biopharmaceutical companies are organized structurally by major functions, such as research and development (R&D), sales, and manufacturing. The ability to organize around smaller slices of business such as cardiology or Alzheimer's disease is offset by the synergies of manufacturing multiple products in a few plants, or managing all clinical trials under one global group. Whereas these large functions of R&D, sales, and manufacturing have their own economies of scale, the ability to collaborate across these large functions is quite difficult. Many of the large pharmaceutical companies have tried to create smaller franchises by customer group or therapeutic area; however, these are typically just committees, with the budgets remaining in the major functions. Hence, the challenge of getting multiple, big, cross-purposed but interdependent functions to work together and share goals continues to be a struggle at nearly all biopharma companies today.

Exhibit 7.1 shows the basic core processes required to bring a medicine to patients.

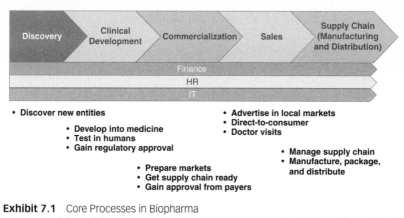

Exhibit 7.1 Core Processes in Biopharma
Source: Medicines Differentiation Analytics, LLC, 2013. All rights reserved. Patent pending.

- ■ **Discovery.** Scientists are performing various tests to uncover or innovate new potential medicines. All of this is done preclinically or before a medicine is tested in humans. The challenges in this phase are the high attrition rates (many failed projects) and high cost.

- ■ **Clinical development.** The potential medicine is tested in humans. In a phase 1 trial, the potential medicine is tested in a very small group of people. First, in a phase 1a trial, the medicine is tested on a small group of healthy individuals to ensure that it has no harmful effect. Then, in a phase 1b trial, the medicine is tested on a small group of sick patients to see if it actually works as planned. Subsequently, a phase 2 trial allows various doses of the medicine to be tested in a relatively small population of patients to find the optimum dose. If all is successful, a phase 3 trial is begun. In this trial, the medicine is tested on a much larger sample of sick patients and often for a longer duration. At the end of a successful phase 3 trial, the data on the medicine is given to an approval body (such as the Food and Drug Administration [FDA]) for approval.

    Meanwhile, during these phases of development, the drug is manufactured in small batches for the clinical trials and a scalable manufacturing process is designed.

Challenges in development are the long cycle times within and between the phases, the high cost to manufacture the clinical supplies, and attrition rates.

■ **Commercialization.** There are significant activities that must be done to get a drug launched. Obviously, manufacturing must prepare to scale up from the small batches during the clinical trials to a fully functioning manufacturing plant meeting the required volumes from day one of launch. In addition, the commercial groups are working to get the payer community to provide access and pay for their new drugs over other alternatives. In addition, each country is getting involved to prepare its market for the new drug (educating doctors, advertising direct to consumers, etc.). A great challenge is incurring a successful launch whereby as close to peak sales are experienced on day one. With the patent end looming, any day with slow sales is truly a waste. A perfect launch has the right medicine in the right place meeting predicted demand in an environment ready for the drug.

■ **Sales.** The sales model in all of the biopharma industry is changing dramatically. The traditional model of "boots on the streets" is no longer viable due both to doctors not having time and to restrictions placed on sales representatives. Consequently, companies are finding ways to use technology and social media to reach both prescribers and patients.

■ **Supply chain (manufacturing and distribution).** Finding efficiency in the supply chain processes in biopharma has been a focus since the early 1990s. Many of the companies are adopting lean manufacturing and six sigma principles to drive efficiencies. Complexity in the supply chain begins with the manufacture of the active product ingredient (API) in a facility in one part of the world; then, in a facility in another part of the world, the API is made into a form that is able to be injected or swallowed or absorbed; ultimately, the medicine is packaged in a plant in the United States and shipped out to wholesalers for distribution. Often a new facility is built to handle the new demand and quality considerations of the new medicine. In addition to being complex, the biopharma supply chain around the world has significant overcapacity issues. It is a highly capital-intensive, high-cost, and underutilized environment.

Last, support functions such as finance, information technology (IT), and human resources (HR) support the core functions as they do in other industries. However, often in the biopharma industry there are dedicated functions for each core function. For example, an IT group is dedicated to R&D with little alignment to company-wide IT activities. This makes it harder to gain synergies across IT, HR, and finance globally in these situations.

CASE STUDIES

The following case studies demonstrate real examples of how applying predictive business analytics with more predictable performance measures can drive new behaviors and results.

- Case Study A, customer-driven predictive performance analytics for predicting a medicine's success in the market.
- Case Study B, new measures to drive new Learn & Confirm R&D model.

Case Study A: Customer-Driven Predictive Performance Analytics to Differentiate and Predict a Medicine's Success in the Market

One of the most challenging decisions facing biopharmaceutical companies is whether to invest in potential new drugs. Failure rates during late stage development can be as high as 50 percent. And failure rates after regulatory approval are now plaguing the industry as never before. Such examples include:

- An approved blockbuster drug that moved a daily injection to inhalation (assumed much more convenient for patients)—yet insurance companies saw no efficacious benefit and would not provide access or reimbursement.
- The years wasted by one pharmaceutical company trying to get payer approval for reimbursement, only to subsequently find out that patients are happy to pay for the lifestyle medicine themselves.

■ An addictive habit cessation drug that obtained approval and access, but patients preferred cold turkey withdrawal than to take a drug.

These examples demonstrate the changing environment in medicine commercialization, with multiple decision makers all playing a role. The decision to continue investing in a medicine is more difficult today than ever before. When we factor in the reduced R&D budgets and the move to personalized medicines (versus blockbusters), this challenge only grows exponentially.

As a result, one large biopharmaceutical giant realized (after experiencing many market failures) that just getting a potential medicine over regulatory approval (FDA or other global body) is no longer the only hurdle. Now, success in the market means the potential drug will be:

■ *Granted access and paid for* over other treatments.

■ *Prescribed* over alternative treatments.

■ *Taken* over other treatments.

■ *Approved* over alternative treatments.

It is no longer good enough to get medicines approved by the FDA or similar global bodies. For example, a medicine may be efficacious and safe enough to gain regulatory approval, but may not be taken by patients due to convenience or pain management issues. In addition, often approved drugs are not accepted by insurance companies and therefore not provided access to patients or reimbursed for because they are too expensive when a generic alternative is just as good.

These challenges will continue to get worse as new health care laws are put in place.

The challenge: to predict early on (pre–phase 3) the likelihood a medicine will be:

■ Approved.

■ Paid for.

■ Prescribed.

■ Taken over all other alternatives.

How can we begin to predict success before investing significant amounts of money?

In response, this company embarked on developing and implementing *customer-driven predictive differentiation analytics.* The definition of *customer* in this case includes patients, payers, prescribers, caregivers, and approvers. Customer-driven predictive differentiation analytics scores inform a user how much better one treatment option is over another and why. It has significant uses for different markets:

- Patients in a conversation about treatment options with their doctors.
- Biopharma investment committees deciding whether to continue investment in a potential compound.
- Health care insurance companies deciding whether to reimburse a new medicine at a higher rate due to its positive differentiation against other treatments.

Using MedifVu, a predictive methodology and database, customer value statements were obtained and converted into outcome measures, and ultimately customer-driven differentiation scores were calculated. Beginning with outcome measures important to all customer groups, clinical data outcomes are displayed on a continuum from bad to good.

Exhibit 7.2 depicts the process by which customer-driven differentiation scores are developed.

Customer Value Statement

Drug development traditionally is not a customer-driven process. Other industries that develop new products within months can be aligned nearly immediately to the changing needs of the customers. But within biopharmaceuticals, when drug development spans at least 10 years, the ability to tie products directly to changing customer needs is truly a challenge. While we may not be able to modify a new diabetes medicine to the desires of patients, we can compare different diabetes treatments pros and cons to what is important to patients.

For example, success for a multiple sclerosis (MS) drug may be measured by the drug development scientist as a reduced number of relapses that occur in a year, yet to the MS patient success may mean

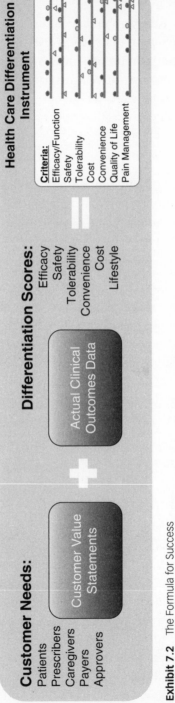

Exhibit 7.2 The Formula for Success

Source: Medicines Differentiation Analytics, LLC, 2013. All rights reserved. Patent pending.

the ability to walk a mile during the day. Without correct customer value statements, we will not be measuring what our customers (patients, caregivers, payers, prescribers) care about.

Customer value statements are summarized into categories such as efficacy, safety, convenience, lifestyle, cost, and so on. By knowing and measuring outcomes directly tied to customer value statements, we can more easily predict whether a new medicine will be taken, approved, paid for, and approved over alternatives.

Customer-Driven Predictive Differentiation Scores

Based on the outcome measures obtained in the customer value statements, the results of current in-line and pipeline products are plotted on a measurable continuum from good to bad. This display can highlight strengths and weaknesses of a particular drug, thereby predicting its ultimate strength in the market. Having this data early on can highlight to decision makers whether to continue investing in a compound into phase 3, or even earlier into phase 1. Exhibit 7.3 is an example of differentiation scores.

A differentiation score is calculated for each in-line or pipeline product based on where the product sits on the continuum against other pipeline and in-line products. In this example, the in-line medicine denoted by the larger black ovals has the greatest market differentiation

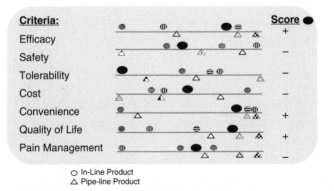

Exhibit 7.3 Integrated Health Care Differentiation Scores
Source: Medicines Differentiation Analytics, LLC, 2013. All rights reserved. Patent pending.

above other competing alternatives in the area of convenience—and is most negatively differentiated for tolerability.

Application in Biopharma

For this case study company, its investment committees used this analysis to determine whether the company should continue to invest in a potential treatment. For example, one can begin to predict that one of the drugs in the pipeline, noted in the white triangle, will not have a strong position of differentiation in the market, and continued investment in it should be questioned. This company's investment boards used this predictive business analysis at key milestones such as phase 1, phase 2, and phase 3 decisions. Investment in potential drugs without strong differentiation was halted from further development, or trials were redirected to show differentiation in at least one very key area.

Using this type of predictive business analysis limits the ability of one function such as safety to drive decision making solely on what it believes is important. The drug may be very safe, but may not have the convenience or lifestyle support that other decision makers care about. For biopharmaceutical companies, getting all functions (regulatory, safety, clinical, commercial, access, finance) to come together, be aligned, and view such analysis is the key to success.

In addition, predictive differentiation analysis changed the dynamics and structure of the case study company's drug development committees. Originally, the company had one committee for development and another for commercialization. This analysis requires both parties to be present, hence reducing the need for two committees.

Application in the Health Care Payer Community

Beyond this case study example, other stakeholders in health care can benefit from predictive differentiation analytics. Health care insurance providers are continually questioning one treatment's advantage over another. Should they provide access to that treatment for their patients, and, if they do, at what price? This analysis provides objective comparative measurements to decide on whether access should be granted and at what premium given how differentiated that potential new medicine might be.

Application to Providers, Caregivers, and Patients

In addition, the data is pushed to mobile devices, allowing patients, caregivers, and doctors to evaluate treatment options in a mobile setting. Patients can even add their medical histories or preferences to further tailor the treatment options to them.

This display provides the foundation for a robust conversation between patient and physician to discuss treatment pros and cons unique for that patient (see Exhibit 7.4).

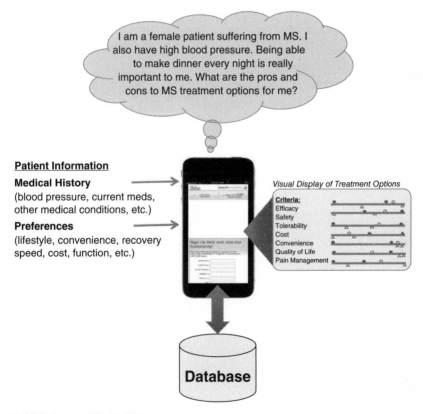

Exhibit 7.4 Mobile MedifVu
Source: Medicines Differentiation Analytics, LLC, 2013. All rights reserved. Patent pending.

Additional Predictive Business Analytics

Once customer-driven predictive scores are obtained, depending on the user and the decision required, additional analysis includes:

- **Predicted differentiated label claims.** What is the exact wording required on the label to claim differentiation for approval, marketing, and pricing purposes?
- **Payer behavior.** Based on prior actions, how likely is the payer community to provide access and higher pricing for this new medicine?
- **Real/win/worth analysis.** Ultimately, all these predictive analytics culminate into analysis of:
  - How *real* the opportunity is (size of market and strength of customer need).
  - The likelihood whether this product can *win* in the market (how uniquely differentiated it is).
  - And if it is *worth* the journey in terms of either financial, reputation, or other reasons.

As all of these analyses come together, we can predict with greater certainty the likelihood this new medicine will be:

- *Approved* over other treatments.
- *Paid for and granted access* over alternative treatments.
- *Prescribed* over other treatments.
- *Taken* over alternative treatments.

The potential benefits for organizing a capability and capacity to foster customer-driven predictive differentiation analytics in biopharmaceuticals have never been timelier:

- The Patient **Protection and Affordable Care Act** is requiring comparative effectiveness analysis of treatment options.
- The **Patient-Centered Outcomes Research Institute (PCORI)** is pushing for clinical trials focused on outcome measures important to patients.
- **Biopharma R&D budgets** are shrinking while the need for new treatments and innovation has never been stronger.

■ The explosion of use of **mobile devices** cannot be ignored in the engagement of patients and caregivers in their treatments.

Summary

This case study highlights why and how the use of key performance metrics such as customer value statements and differentiation scores can be vital to predict future success of a potential product. It illustrates in the biopharma industry that knowing the size of the potential market is only one piece of the predictive business analysis capability. But knowing how a product sits competitively against its current and future competition along metrics important to the buying customer is the real measure for predicting market success. With all decision makers weighing in, there will be a higher probability the new medicine will be:

■ *Approved* over alternatives.

■ *Provided access and reimbursement* over alternatives.

■ *Prescribed* and *taken* over all other alternatives.

The case also serves as an example that can be applied to many other industries facing similar challenges, market conditions, regulatory oversight, and constrained resources.

Case Study B: New Measures to Drive New Learn & Confirm R&D Model

A $22 billion global biopharmaceutical company gained a new CEO and embarked on shaking up the sleeping giant. Every function and division across the company was asked to embrace change and challenge everything it was doing. The CEO was new to the biopharmaceutical world, but understood its challenges of price decreases, heightened competition, and major patent losses. If other industries can do it, so will a biopharmaceutical.

The head of R&D embraced this challenge. He created a task force to study new ways to get business done, even ways outside their industry. The team came upon published articles on "Learn & Confirm." Dr. Lewis Sheiner first introduced the concept in 1997 in his landmark article in *Clinical Pharmacology & Therapeutics*.[1]

Conceptually, the Learn & Confirm model states that to establish a molecule's proof of concept requires significant learning, risk taking, and experiments on that molecule to fully understand how and why it works. This experimental risk-taking phase is called the Learn phase. Then, once proof of concept has clearly been established in the Learn phase, attention shifts to the speed and cost at which we can confirm our molecule hypothesis. Therefore, focus during the Confirm phase is on ensuring that the regulated clinical trials are met efficiently and effectively, as well as quickly. The Confirm phase typically begins at the start of a phase 3 trial.

After much research and debate, this company began to understand how Learn & Confirm could apply to its biopharmaceutical business, culture, and organizational structure.

Prior to the new model, the current drug development process is a series of handoffs from many different groups (discovery, development, commercial), with significant input from such groups as regulatory, safety, finance, and so on.

Exhibit 7.5 shows the typical traditional process from "New Application" to a big "Phase 3 decision" to "Launch." As expected, large organizations are involved and big handoffs result. There is no doubt that quality and cycle time to market are critical performance measures in this process.

The major handoff adds unneeded cycle time to a process already taking too long to get to market. Worse is often the dreaded "high five at regulatory (approval)," referring to when the R&D organization celebrates at FDA approval, then hands the medicine to the sales department to go sell it, and seemingly walks away from any ownership of it. The R&D organization will get rewarded for achieving FDA approval, even if the product never sells one pill.

As you can see, the performance measures used tend to focus on events each separate organization can control, and all are measured on cost and cycle time.

In Exhibit 7.6, the Learn & Confirm model greatly shifts to allow the early stage work (prior to a big Phase 3 study) to be all about Learning and after that to be all about Confirming they were right.

In the new Learn & Confirm model, there is a new way of thinking about the process of bringing medicines to market.

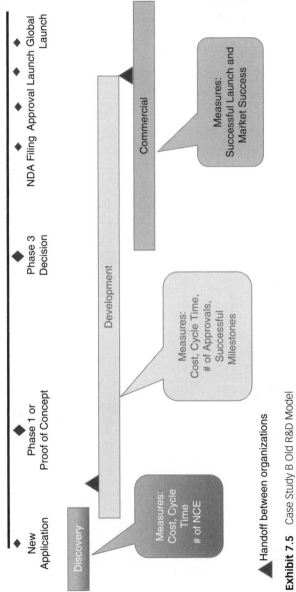

Exhibit 7.5 Case Study B Old R&D Model

Source: Medicines Differentiation Analytics, LLC, 2013. All rights reserved. Patent pending.

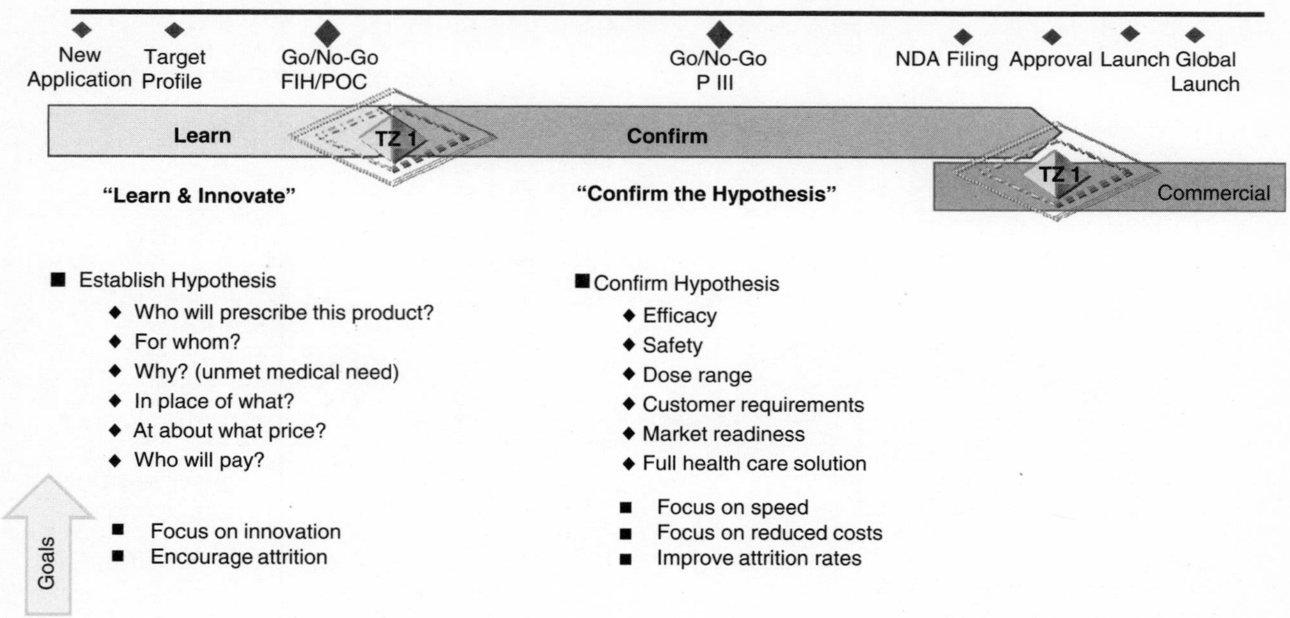
New Application
Target Profile
Go/No-Go FIH/POC
Go/No-Go P III
NDA Filing
Approval
Launch
Global Launch
Learn
TZ 1
Confirm
TZ 1
Commercial
"Learn & Innovate"
"Confirm the Hypothesis"
Establish Hypothesis
Who will prescribe this product?
For whom?
Why? (unmet medical need)
In place of what?
At about what price?
Who will pay?
Confirm Hypothesis
Efficacy
Safety
Dose range
Customer requirements
Market readiness
Full health care solution
Goals
Focus on innovation
Encourage attrition
Focus on speed
Focus on reduced costs
Improve attrition rates

Exhibit 7.6 Case Study B New R&D Model

Source: Medicines Differentiation Analytics, LLC, 2013. All rights reserved. Patent pending.

First there is the Learn phase; here the focus is on learning, being innovative, taking risks, and making mistakes. From Discovery to a phase 3 decision, the scientists are encouraged to innovate. They are no longer rewarded only based on costs, cycle times, or events. At this stage, the company encourages high attrition rates (rates of failed medicines). Now is the time to weed out the drugs that will fail, before the company has invested significant money in them.

Then there is the Confirm phase; after a positive investment decision is made to move into a costly phase 3 trial, the focus now shifts to speed and low cost. We now want the team to focus on project management and proving the hypothesis. We should not be taking additional risks here. Phase 3 trials are very expensive and long. Anything we can do to speed up the trials while reaching our regulatory approval goals is the new focus. Attrition (failures) is not accepted at this point (due to the investment costs). It is key that during the Learn phase, we truly learned what we needed to, so that the probability of failure during the Confirm phase should be minimal.

In the handoffs between Learn & Confirm, there are transition zones. Transition zones require combined teams so that history and knowledge are not lost and that a smooth transition to the new team occurs. Often a Learn team member may stay on the new Confirm team.

In addition to unique performance measures between Learn & Confirm teams, the required skills of team members will be very different. Learn teams encourage people who love to innovate and take risks. Confirm teams encourage people who are great at execution, communication, and project management—people who get things done in a timely fashion and within budget.

Challenges to Implementation

To implement the new model required nearly every function of the company's involvement. Perhaps only the true sales organization focused on doctors and hospitals was not directly affected. This implementation required the attention of such organizations as regulatory, project management, senior decision-making bodies, scientists, HR, and safety.

HR's role is critical, as a new organization structure must emerge. Required skills, performance measures, and career tracks between people in Learn versus Confirm will be widely different and must be established.

Governance boards not only need to be engaged, but are quite often redesigned to ensure the right focus between the Learn versus Confirm phases. How the board members ask questions and what they expect from a Learn team will be vastly different from what they expect from a Confirm team. Educating and/or redesigning governance boards to fit the new model must be addressed.

Educating teams on the changing expectations is key. Encouraging and rewarding failures and risk taking in the Learn phase may feel uncomfortable to teams at first, while questioning risk taking and cycle time delays during the Confirm phase must become part of the dialogue.

Overcoming corporate culture steeped in major functions not knowing (and perhaps not caring) what the other function is doing is once again a big challenge. While there is no silver bullet, strong leadership, clear and consistent messaging, and addressing the "what's in it for me?" question are critical ingredients for success.

- **Leadership.** Leaders must visibly and actively demonstrate their belief in the new Learn & Confirm model—not just in written form but in the language that they use in all forums (town halls, department meetings, and one-on-ones). They set the tone for success.

- **Communication.** Employees need to understand what the new model is, and how they fit in it. Messaging must come in all forms. And the best is from their direct boss, letting his or her direct reports know that the boss believes in this, supports it, and wants them to also. People usually do what their boss asks them to, not what some boss's boss or an outside consultant said. Cascading communications down into every department meeting by that department head can be the most effective piece of the puzzle.

- **What's in it for me?** Communication must address how everyone (good or bad) will be affected by the change. Nearly all transitions have silver linings for all involved. Emphasizing those silver linings, or the new opportunities the transition opens up, or the new roles available, or the potential career paths will help people begin to see how they can benefit from the new world. Clearly, the new Learn & Confirm model provided tremendous opportunity for people to drive their careers in a slightly different, yet perhaps more effective and rewarding way.

SUMMARY

In this second case study, the new Learn & Confirm philosophy and methodology, which is embedded in the predictive business analytics capabilities of this company, has reshaped the governance focus across drug development and provided a new shared language across multiple functions. As a result, attrition rates (failures) in Confirm (phase 3) have reduced significantly. This is attributed to the efforts of learning all that the company can about the molecule before it considers investing significant dollars in a phase 3 trial.

As with the previous case, predictive business analytics can be found in a variety of organizational forms and structures; however, its value contributions are real and sustaining.

NOTE

1. Lewis B. Sheiner, "Learning versus Confirming in Clinical Drug Development," *Clinical Pharmacology & Therapeutics* 61 (March 1997): 275–291.

PART FOUR

Integrating Business Methods and Techniques

CHAPTER 8

Why Do Companies Fail (Because of Irrational Decisions)?

The time to repair the roof is when the sun is shining.

—John F. Kennedy

There are numerous examples of large, once-successful companies that have failed. They have gone bankrupt or substantially reduced in size and fallen from an industry leadership position. Examples include Wang Labs, Digital Equipment, Borders, and Blockbuster. What has caused their failures? Is it possible that they were not sufficiently analytical? Might the explanation be that they had adequate information and analysis but made irrational decisions?

IRRATIONAL DECISION MAKING

Dr. Franck Schuurmans, a guest lecturer at the Wharton Business School and a consultant for Decision Strategies International, has captivated audiences with explanations of why people make irrational business decisions. A simple exercise he uses in his lectures is to provide a list of 10 questions, such as "In what year was Mozart born?" The task is to select a range of possible answers such that you have 90 percent confidence that the correct answer falls in your chosen range. Mozart was born in 1756, so, for example, you could narrowly select 1730 to 1770, or you could more broadly select 1600 to 1900. The range is your choice. Surprisingly, the vast majority choose correctly for no more than five of the 10 questions. Why so bad? Most choose too narrow bounds. The lesson is that people have an innate desire to be correct despite no penalty for being wrong.

Schuurmans's research goes deeply into the nuances of cognitive psychology and the theories of bounded rationality that earned Herbert Simon the Nobel Prize in economics in 1978. A key observation is that humans have limited rationality between our ears—our brains were designed to hunt prey. Typically, people defer to mental shortcuts from learning by discovery. The academic term is *heuristics*. For example, as was described in framing a problem in Chapter 1, a man decides to take an umbrella if the sky has dark clouds, but not if it is sunny. The clouds are probably enough for the umbrella decision— but is he 100 percent sure it will rain? Perhaps not, but the degree of certainty is probably good enough for the umbrella decision. But do you know or just think you know? This is an example of the limits of decision making. Mental shortcuts, gut feel, intuition, and so on typically work—until problems get complex. I will return to this topic of complex problems, but first let's discuss reasons why companies fail.

WHY DO LARGE, SUCCESSFUL COMPANIES FAIL?

Companies may feel invulnerable today but be aimless tomorrow. Do companies fail because their problems and opportunities have become very complex but they address them with insufficient information to make decisions (like taking an umbrella or not)?

We should all be intrigued by the fact that almost half of the 25 companies that passed the rigorous tests for inclusion in Tom Peters and Robert Waterman's 1982 book, *In Search of Excellence*,[1] today either no longer exist, are in bankruptcy, or have performed poorly. What happened in the 30 years since the book was published?

And consider this: Of the original Standard & Poor's (S&P) 500 list created in 1957, just 74, only 15 percent, are on that list today, according to research from Professor Gary Biddle of the University of Hong Kong. Of those 74, only 12 have outperformed the S&P index average. Pretty grim. A few years from now will the popular book, *Good to Great*, by Jim Collins[2] reveal the praised companies in the book as laggards?

Perhaps the explanation is that when an organization is enjoying success, it breeds adversity to taking wise and calculated risks. The executives are too confident that what has worked in the past will continue to work in the future. But each new day requires making strategic adjustments to anticipate continuously changing customer needs and countertactics by competitors. Predictive analytics is used to develop customer microsegments to increase sales conversion rates and reduce defections to competitors by offering the right product, service, or promotion at the right price at the right time.

Risk management is about balancing risk appetite with risk exposure. If there is not enough risk-taking appetite, then performance will eventually suffer. (If the risk appetite is excessive, though—well, the recent global financial crisis is evidence of its outcome.) How can an organization create sustainability for its long-term performance? What role might embracing predictive business analytics play in mitigating risks and providing a competitive edge?

In Sydney Finkelstein's book *Why Smart Executives Fail*,[3] he observes that the cause of failure is not lack of intelligence—executives are typically quite smart. Failure is not necessarily due to unforeseeable events, either. Companies that have failed often knew what was happening but chose not to do much about it. Nor is failure always the result of taking the wrong daily actions. Finkelstein's explanation involves the attitude of executives. This includes a breakdown in their reasoning and strategic thinking as well as a failure to create a culture for metrics and deep analysis.

As mentioned, prominent examples of failure are Wang Labs and Digital Equipment. Wang Labs failed in part because it specialized in computers designed exclusively for word processing and did not foresee general-purpose personal computers (PCs) with word processing software in the 1980s, mainly developed by IBM. Digital Equipment was satisfied with its dominance in the core minicomputer market, which it was first to introduce. However, Digital was slow to adapt its product line to the new markets for personal computers. The company's entry into the PC arena in 1982 was a failure, and later PC collaborations with Olivetti and Intel achieved mixed results.

Often no one challenges the status quo and asks the tough questions. Delusion and fear of the unknown can develop, affecting how organizations handle key relationships with customers and suppliers. When it comes to considering whether to adopt advanced business analytics, or whether to implement and integrate the various component methodologies that constitute analytics-based enterprise performance management (EPM), there are actually two choices: to do it or not to do it. Many organizations ignore the fact that the choice *not* to act, which means to continue with the status quo and to perpetuate making decisions the way they currently are doing, is *also* a decision.

In many cases, executives believe that if there is a control system in place, it will do the job for which it was intended. However, in many organizations, the systems and policies are constructed for day-to-day transactions but not for robustly analyzing the abundance of raw data to make sense of it all. Sustainability is based on transforming data into analyzable information for insights and foresight to improve decision making. This is where business intelligence, predictive business analytics, and analytics-based enterprise performance management systems fit in.

FROM DATA TO INSIGHTS

The transformation from data to insights has four phases:

Phase 1: Data. Data is raw information that has not been processed or prioritized.

Phase 2: Information. Information is select facts that are of interest but lack implications.

Phase 3: Understanding. Understanding creates knowledge and begins to get at the how and the why, but it fails to suggest action.

Phase 4: Insight. Insight is actionable intelligence that is derived from a variety of sources. Insight provides a holistic view of a problem and its solution.

Analytics applies in phases 3 and 4. One knows that they have achieved actionable insight when an "aha" results, the situation is relatively easy to understand, and one can project the impact of taking the action.

INCREASING THE RETURN ON INVESTMENT FROM INFORMATION ASSETS

Schuurmans observed that mental shortcuts work *except* when problems become complex. When problems do get complex, then a new set of issues arises. Systematic thinking is required. What often trips people up is that they do not start by framing a problem before they begin collecting information that will lead to their conclusions. There is often a bias or preconception. One seeks data that will validate one's bias. The adverse effect, as Schuurmans describes it, is "We prepare ourselves for X, and Y happens." By framing a problem, one widens the options to formulate hypotheses.

How is this relevant for applying predictive business analytics, the emerging field of interest to improve organizational performance? A misconception to information technology specialists is that they equate applying business intelligence (BI) technologies with query and reporting techniques such as data mining or collect large troves of data such as "Big Data" and assume that meaningful insights will present themselves.

In practice, experienced analysts do not use BI as if they were searching for a diamond in a coal mine. They don't flog the data until it confesses with the truth. Instead, they first speculate that two or more things are related or that some underlying behavior is driving a pattern seen in various data. They apply business analytics more for confirmation than for random exploration. This requires analysts to have easy and flexible access to data, the ability to manipulate the data, and software to support their investigative process.

Without initial problem framing and a confirmatory approach, mistakes are inevitable. Sadly, as Schuurmans observed, many do not learn from their mistakes, but repeat them with more gusto.

In his book *Predictably Irrational*,[4] author Dan Ariely observes, "We are all far less rational in our decision making than standard economic theory assumes. Our irrational behaviors are neither random nor senseless—they are systematic and predictable. So wouldn't economics make a lot more sense if it were based on how people actually behave? That simple idea is the basis of behavioral economics."

One can expand on Ariely's observation by asking a comparable question: Wouldn't getting a return on investment from an organization's treasure trove of stored raw and transactional data be greater and more meaningful if we properly applied predictive business analytics? The main takeaway here is that organizations that embrace evidenced-based decision making shift the mix from predominantly emotional to rational decision making.

The author Mark Twain said, "It ain't what you don't know that gets you into trouble. It's what you know for sure that just ain't so."

EMERGING NEED FOR ANALYTICS

With today's gradual recovery from the global recession triggered in 2008, the stakes have never been higher for managers to make better, faster decisions with analyzable information. Companies that successfully use their information will out-think, outsmart, and out-execute their competitors. High-performing enterprises are building their strategies around information-driven insights that generate results from the power of analytics of all flavors, such as segmentation and regression analysis, and especially predictive business analytics. They are proactive, not reactive.

A *Harvard Business Review* article[5] sheds additional light on the topic of complexity. It notes the difference between something being merely complicated and being genuinely complex. Think of systems. Complicated systems have many moving parts, like a wristwatch with gears; but they operate in patterned ways. In contrast, complex systems have patterned ways, but the interactions—think variables—are continually changing. In the former one can usually predict outcomes. The math may be easy with linear relationships. In the latter, like with air traffic control, weather and aircraft maintenance delays cause changes in the constant interactions with numerous variables. To make better decisions, the modeling and analytics need to be adaptive and flexible. They need to have self-learning capabilities to get increasingly smarter.

Executives are human and can make mistakes, but in company failures, these are not simply minor misjudgments. In many cases, their errors are enormous miscalculations that can be explained by problems in leadership. Regardless of how decentralized some businesses might claim to be in their decision making, corporations can be rapidly brought to the brink of failure by executives whose personal qualities create risks rather than mitigate them. In Finkelstein's book, he observes that these flaws can be honorable—such as with CEOs like An Wang of Wang Labs—or less than honorable, as was the case with rogue CEOs such as Dennis Kozlowski of Tyco, Ken Lay of Enron, John Rigas of Adelphia, and Steve Hilbert of Conseco.

To sustain long-term success, companies need leaders with vision and inspiration to answer "Where do we want to go?" Then, by communicating their strategy to managers and employees, they can empower their workforce with analytical tools to correctly answer "How will we get there?" This goes to the heart of analytics and especially forward-looking predictive analytics. As was earlier mentioned in Chapter 1 about strategic versus operational decisions, employees make hundreds, possibly thousands, of decisions every day, such as pricing, customer targeting, and freight distribution routing. Incrementally better small decisions add up and may contribute more to the financial bottom-line impact than the few big decisions made by executives.

SUMMARY

There are hundreds of books already written about leadership and hundreds that remain to be written. One would think that by now, with all lessons learned about which leadership style works best, there would be a simple instruction manual. But of course we all know it is not that simple. Leadership is much more art than it is science or even a craft.

In this chapter we learned that a leading cause for failure in organizations is the attitude of executives. Some executives will rely on their instincts that their intuition and career experiences have provided rather than having facts, deep analysis, and relevant insight, which are necessary most often for making good decisions. Some organizations do not foster enough trust between managers and workforce to challenge the status quo and ask tough questions. An additional reason for organizational failure is not clearly seeing the future that lies ahead and planning for it, including making course direction adjustments.

Explanations of failure like these build the business case for predictive business analytics. Without deep analysis and insight by a team of skilled and capable individuals to understand why things happened and to gain forward-looking insight into what might happen, organizations are at risk of decline. And as volatility continues to intensify, along with the removal of boundaries resulting from a digital world, this risk will only increase. Applying predictive business analytics is essential to mitigating the risk of organizational failure.

NOTES

1. Thomas J. Peters and Robert H. Waterman, *In Search of Excellence: Lessons from America's Best-Run Companies* (New York: HarperCollins, 2004).
2. Jim Collins, *Good to Great: Why Some Companies Make the Leap . . . and Others Don't* (New York: HarperBusiness, 2001).
3. Sydney Finkelstein, *Why Smart Executives Fail: And What You Can Learn from Their Mistakes* (New York: Penguin, 2004).
4. Dan Ariely, *Predictably Irrational: The Hidden Forces That Shape Our Decisions* (New York: HarperCollins, 2009).
5. Gockce Sargut and Rita Gunther McGrath, "Learning to Live with Complexity," *Harvard Business Review*, October 2011.

CHAPTER 9

Integration of Business Intelligence, Business Analytics, and Enterprise Performance Management

If you have built castles in the air, your work need not be lost; that is where they should be. Now put foundations under them.

—Henry David Thoreau

Business intelligence is not the same thing as predictive business analytics. Business intelligence is mainly about querying, drilling down into detail, and reporting. In contrast, analytics addresses understanding the "why" for what has happened, including gaining insights to causes. Predictive business analytics takes an extra step to projecting what can happen in the future.

The late Nobel Prize-winning nuclear physicist Richard Feynman learned a valuable lesson as a child. His father showed him a picture of a bird species and told Feynman its name in several languages—all uniquely different. Then his father noted that regardless of the bird's various names, it did not in any way affect the reality of the bird's existence or its physical features. The lesson for Feynman was that no matter what name people use for something, it does not alter what that something is. We can apply that lesson to the confusion today about the difference between mainstream business intelligence (BI),[1] business analytics (BA), and enterprise performance management (EPM).

Are BI, BA, and EPM different terms for one bird species or for two different birds—or animals? Are BI and BA part of EPM? Or is EPM part of BI and BA?

There is ambiguity since the underlying inputs, processes, outputs, and outcomes of an organization—whether a public-sector government agency or a commercial business—may arguably have some parts that belong to BI and BA, while others belong to EPM. The key word in that sentence is *arguably*. This argument arises because IT-centric people often see an enterprise as a ravenous consumer of billions of bytes of data (what some are calling "big data") intended to manage the business (a BI view). In contrast, leaders, managers, and employee teams typically view the same enterprise as an organism with a purpose and mission (an EPM view); they desire solutions and applications that achieve results. How can BI and BA be reconciled with EPM? The enterprise is like that single species of bird—nothing can change its existence in reality.

RELATIONSHIP AMONG BUSINESS INTELLIGENCE, BUSINESS ANALYTICS, AND ENTERPRISE PERFORMANCE MANAGEMENT

EPM puts BI into context. In essence, BI reporting *consumes* stored data that was cleansed and integrated from disparate source systems and then *transformed* into information. Analytics *produces* new information, and predictive business analytics (PBA) produces new forward-looking information that can be used by management to better understand what is occurring and, as important, what might occur in the future. EPM then *leverages and deploys* the information. EPM requires BI as a foundation. When predictive business analytics is added to BI and EPM, organizations gain insights and foresight for better and faster decision making. That is, in this context information is much more valuable than data points, because integrating and transforming data using calculations and pattern discovery results in potentially meaningful information that can be used for decisions.

The greater the integration of the EPM methodologies and their seasoning with all flavors of analytics, especially predictive business analytics, the greater the power of EPM. Predictive business analytics is important because organizations are shifting from managing by control and reacting to after-the-fact data toward managing with anticipatory planning so they can be proactive, making adjustments and taking corrective actions before problems arise.

For example, an automobile manufacturer's warranty claims can be globally analyzed to detect a design problem. In another instance, the history of an individual's credit card purchase transaction data can be converted to information that, in turn, can be used for decisions by retailers to better serve that customer or provide customized offers to sell more to him or her.

In fact, case examples after case examples have demonstrated that to use PBA effectively a company must commit to a sustained and rigorous process in order to achieve meaningful results. This includes the ability to establish a team of individuals with complementary skills and competencies, a repeatable set of practices, and functional data and tools. Together, these are used to continuously analyze the right drivers and measures that have a strong cause-and-effect relationship to the decisions at hand.

As referenced in the Preface and Chapter 5, in one survey, 90 percent of respondents attained a positive ROI from their most successful deployment of predictive business analytics, and more than half from their *least* successful deployment.[2] In another survey, "Among respondents who have implemented predictive business analytics, 66% say it provides 'very high' or 'high' business value."[3]

Key business decisions need to be made with their likely expectation of outcomes or results. PBA is a backbone to enable more effective decision making that recognizes how the future might play out. Take, for example, Dell, which manages its logistics network and its inventory of components to assemble desktops or notebooks based on customer orders. Its agility is in how it has configured shippable products and the supplier chain necessary to manage components and assembly at an efficient level.

PBA is the technique that links levels of inventory to planned assembly labor capacity to forecasted customer orders in an orderly and (hopefully) cost-efficient manner. At the end, its inventory and assembly are integrated into its total business model, customers receive ordered products in a timely manner, and Dell achieves its targeted operating margins, market share, and customer loyalty.[4]

A survey by the global technology consulting firm Accenture reported that senior U.S. executives are increasingly disenchanted with their current analytic and BI capabilities.[5] Although they acknowledged that their BI (regardless of how they personally define it) provides a display of data in terms of reporting, querying, searching, and visual dashboards, they felt their mainstream BI still fell short. An organization's interest is not just to *monitor* the dials; it is more important to *move* the dials. That is, just reporting information does not equate to managing for better results and decision making; what is needed are inherent organizational capabilities and competencies to define actions and proffer decision alternatives to improve the organization's performance. Having mainstream BI capability is definitely important; however, it often has come about as the result of departments needing advances that their IT function could not provide.

Managing and improving are not the same thing. Many people are managers, like a coach of a sports team, and they get by. *Improving*, in contrast, is how an organization wins. To differentiate BI and PBA from EPM, enterprise performance management can be viewed as *deploying* the power of BI and PBA, but all three are inseparable. Think of EPM as an *application* of BI. EPM adds context and direction for BI. As in physics, BI is like potential energy, while PBA and EPM are the conversion of potential energy into kinetic energy. Coal, when heated, provides power to move things. Using a track-and-field analogy, BI is like the muscle of a pole-vaulter, and PBA and EPM are that same athlete clearing higher heights. BI is an enterprise information platform for querying, reporting, and much more, making it the foundation for effective performance management. PBA and EPM drive the strategy and leverage all of the processes, methodologies, metrics, and systems that monitor, manage, and, most important, *improve* enterprise performance. Together, BI, PBA, and EPM form the bridge that connects data to information to actions and decisions.

With EPM, the strategy spurs the application of technology, methodologies, and software. As methodologies—which are typically implemented or operated in isolation from each other—are integrated, the strength and power of BA and EPM grow. Technologies, such as software, support the methodologies. Software is an essential enabler, but the critical part is in the thinking. That is, one must understand the assumptions used in configuring commercial software and, more important, have a vision of the emerging possibilities to apply the new knowledge that BI, PBA, and EPM produce.

OVERCOMING BARRIERS

Many organizations have already begun with basic levels of EPM. Their challenge now is to move up to higher stages of maturity that include integrating EPM's methodologies and embedding analytics into them. See Exhibit 4.1 in Chapter 4 that illustrates an organization's PBA maturity capabilities. A key consideration to expanding an organization's journey is to recognize that the barriers and obstacles are no longer *technical* ones, but rather *social and cultural* ones. These include human nature's resistance to change, fear of being measured and held accountable, and weak leadership. Hence, behavioral change management is a key to realizing value from EPM (see Chapters 12 and 13). Two considerations for the executive team are to create a culture for metrics and applying analytics, and to remove any fear that employees have of reprisals from what is discovered.

Like the bird that Richard Feynman's father described, we should not waste valuable energy debating BI versus Big Data versus PBA versus EPM—we may get caught up in semantics. Rather, we should progress to where PBA and EPM deploy the power in BI with its enterprise information platform so that organizations can advance from managing to improving their performance.

But overcoming barriers that slow the adoption rate of applying analytics is not easy. There are many such barriers, including technical issues such as impure data quality, disparate data sources, and a poorly planned information technology infrastructure. These obstacles can be overcome. The tougher challenge involves the behavior of people, creating a culture for curiosity, and relying on fact-based, data-driven information for investigation to solve problems and pursue opportunities.

Resistance to change is inherent in our human nature. People are comfortable with and like the status quo. The acceptance of analytics to tackle issues related to big data is going through growing pains. The transition pits skeptics, who are typically older and shaped by managing when errors were tolerated, against typically younger enthusiasts who recognize that work environments will require better understanding of processes and outcomes and will involve holding workers accountable with consequences. The margin for error is thinner now.

During the careers of enthusiasts, firefighting has not been an occasional need—it has been ongoing and never-ending. And its intensity is not just because there are more problems (although there are). It is because there are more opportunities requiring a sense of urgency. Enthusiasts' curiosity about how things work is arguably comparable to the older skeptics' when they were the same age. However, the difference is that today the enthusiasts have much greater ability to investigate, analyze, and predict—and with more computing power and more functional software.

SUMMARY

What we have learned in this chapter is that business intelligence (BI) *consumes* stored information, business analytics *produces* new information from the stored data, and predictive business analytics *produces* new forward-looking information that can be used by management to better understand what is occurring and, as important, what might occur in the future. Many EPM methods provide context to *leverage and deploy* analytics with a purpose, such as improving profits from understanding customers better or improving business processes.

We have learned that the barriers to creating a culture to apply predictive business analytics are numerous and in some cases onerous, but they can be overcome. The majority of the barriers are not technical ones but rather social and behavioral ones. That is, information technology and the skills to manage it are less of an issue, so the focus for barrier removal shifts to requiring the soft skills of change management addressed in Chapter 13.

These observations bring us back to leadership (see Chapter 8) as an important factor to foster and drive transformational change, including gaining competency and mastery of applying predictive business analytics.

NOTES

1. The information technology community distinguishes between "little" business intelligence for query and reporting and "big" business intelligence for the platform where information is stored and managed. This chapter's emphasis is on the latter.
2. Predictive Analytics World survey: www.predictiveanalyticsworld.com/Predictive-Analytics-World-Survey-Report-Feb-2009.pdf.
3. Wayne Eckerson, "Predictive Analytics: Extending the Value of Your Data Warehousing Investment," TDWI Report.
4. Adapted from an article by L. S. Maisel, "Cupcakes or Panini?," *Business Finance*, May 2012.
5. Accenture.com, 2005 News Release, "Companies Need to Improve Business Intelligence Capabilities to Drive Growth, Accenture Study Finds."

CHAPTER 10

Predictive Accounting and Marginal Expense Analytics

Business more than any other occupation is a continual dealing with the future; it is a continual calculation, an instructive exercise in foresight.

—Henry R. Luce

There is a growing desire by organizations to understand their costs and the behavior of what drives their costs. An organization's managerial accounting system design can help or hinder its organization's journey toward completing the full vision of enterprise performance management (EPM). It is understandable that people with nonfinancial backgrounds and training have difficulty understanding accounting—for many, accounting is outside their comfort zone.

But there is a gathering storm in the community of management accountants where a need for so-called *advanced* accounting techniques (e.g., activity-based costing management, resource consumption accounting, lean accounting, time-driven activity-based costing) is confusing even the trained accountants, and even seasoned practitioners. The result is that managers and employees receive mixed messages about what costs are the *correct* costs. Upon closer inspection, various costing methods do not necessarily compete. They can coexist and be reconciled and combined. They are all cut from the same cloth; they measure the consumption of economic resources.

LOGIC DIAGRAMS DISTINGUISH BUSINESS FROM COST DRIVERS

Before discussing managerial accounting methods, it is relevant to distinguish business drivers from the cost drivers that eventually monetize information about an organization's expense structure though modeling.

Business drivers may be qualitative or quantitative. For example, for some industries the weather may influence customer demand. An imminent storm will affect consumer purchases and cause hardware stores to stock up on emergency supplies. The severity of the storm may be classified qualitatively, such as high, medium, or low. Eventually the analyst must quantify its impact into unit volume demand quantities. This conversion plus other assumptions will impact inventory management replenishment and open store hour decisions. These in turn are monetized by financial analysts.

The basic message is that business drivers come first and are eventually converted into cost drivers. In activity-based costing systems they are referred to as activity driver cost rates.

Exhibit 10.1 illustrates a popular method of forecasting outcomes referred to as logic diagrams or logic decomposition trees.

In this example the call center selling process to determine the ultimate revenues and profits is derived from a series of logical "if-then" relationships. It begins with estimating the total universe of customers or consumers who will respond to a marketing campaign and initiate a phone call. Subsequent estimates are assumed for conversion outcomes that ultimately allow for monetizing the revenues and products.

There are multiple ways to convert business activities into the language of money. That is the purpose of managerial accounting described in this chapter.

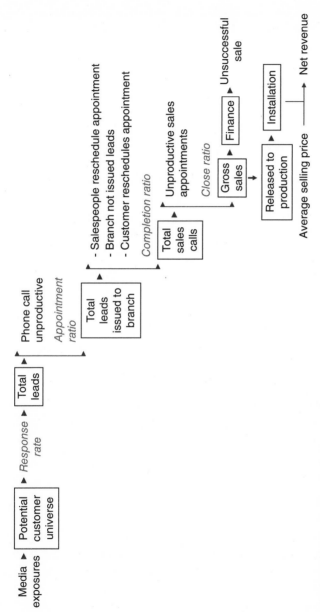

Exhibit 10.1 Predictive Logic Diagrams

149

CONFUSION ABOUT ACCOUNTING METHODS

The fields of law and medicine advance each decade because their bodies of knowledge are codified. Attorneys and physicians stand on the shoulders of their predecessors' captured learning over the centuries. In a sense the generally accepted accounting principles (GAAP) published by the United States' Financial Accounting Standards Board (FASB) and the International Financial Reporting Standards (IFRS) organization have also codified rules and principles. Financial accounting standards support external reporting for government regulatory agencies, bankers, and the investment community.

Unfortunately, unlike financial accounting with its codification, managerial accounting has no such framework or set of universal standards. Accountants are left to their own devices, which are typically the methods and treatments at their organization that they inherit from the prior accountants whom they succeeded. Accountants burn the midnight oil with lots of daily problems to solve, so getting around to improving (or reforming) their organization's management accounting practices and information to benefit their managers and employees is not a frequent occurrence. And the escalation of compliance reporting, such as with Sarbanes-Oxley, is a major distraction from investing time to evaluate improvements to the organization's managerial accounting system.

In the field of accounting, although rules are many, principles are few. Sadly, many accountants were apparently absent from school the day the class defined the purpose of managerial accounting as *to provide data that generates questions, influences people's behavior, and supports good planning, control, and decision making.* Of course, how to apply cost information for decision support can lead to heated debates. For example, what is the incremental cost for taking and delivering one additional customer order? For starters, that answer depends on several assumptions, but if the debaters agree on those assumptions, then the robustness of the costing system and the resulting accuracy requirement to make the correct decision for that question might justify an advanced costing methodology.

Another accounting principle is "precision is a myth"—there is no such thing as a *correct* cost because something's cost is determined (i.e., calculated) based on assumptions that an organization has latitude to make. For example, should we include or exclude a *sunk* cost like equipment depreciation in a product's cost? The answer depends on the type of decision being made. It is this latitude that is causing increasing confusion among accountants. If we step back for a better view, we can see that an organization can refine its managerial accounting system over time through various stages of maturity. Changes to managerial accounting methods and treatments are typically not continuous, and they occur as infrequent and sizably punctuated reforms.

To ensure we are oriented, let us be clear that the topic we are discussing in this chapter is managerial accounting. Under the big umbrella of accounting there is also bookkeeping, financial accounting for external reporting, and tax accounting. Those are peripheral to enterprise performance management. Management accounting information should be viewed as having two broad uses:

1. **A cost autopsy (historical, descriptive).** This information uses cost accounting information for analysis of what already happened in past time periods. The reference to costs as an autopsy is somewhat morbid. However, the money was spent, and cost information reports where did it go. Types of analysis include actual versus budgeted spending for cost variance analysis, activity cost analysis, product profitability, benchmarking, and performance measure monitoring.

2. **Decision support (future, predictive).** This planning and control information serves for economic analysis to support decisions to drive improvement. It involves numerous assumptions such as what-if volume and mix based on projections, and draws on prior economic cost behavior and rates for its calculations. Types of analysis include price and profit margin analysis, capital expenditures, outsourcing decisions, make-or-buy, project evaluation, incremental (or marginal) expense analysis, and rationalization of products, channels, and customers.

To be clear, the higher value-add for performance improvement comes from decision support compared to cost autopsy reporting. And the good news is that the administrative effort of costing for decision support is less because the source information is typically used as needed and for infrequent decisions, such as when setting catalog or list prices, rather than for daily operations. However, some organizations must quote prices daily for custom orders to a wide variety of customers, so it is important that their cost modeling supports profit margin analysis—whether they are on an incremental or a fully absorbed cost basis.

HISTORICAL EVOLUTION OF MANAGERIAL ACCOUNTING

If we travel back through time and revisit the weeks in which an organization's initial *managerial* accounting system was initially architected, we first realize that it is a spin-off or variant of the ongoing *financial* accounting system already in place. The nature of the organization's purpose and the economic conditions it faces govern the initial financial accounting system design. So, for example, if the organization's output is nonrecurring with relatively short product or service life cycles, like constructing a building or executing a consulting engagement, then project accounting is the more appropriate method—a very high form of direct costing. Similarly, if the organization is a manufacturer of unique one-time engineer-to-order products, then it will likely begin with a job-order cost accounting scheme.

In contrast, if the products made or standard service lines delivered (e.g., a bank loan) are continuously recurring, as consequently will also be the associated employee work activities, then the initial financial accounting method may likely take on a standard costing approach (of which activity-based costing is simply a variant). In this case, the repeating material requirements and labor time effort of work tasks are first measured, and then the equivalent costs for both direct material and labor are assumed as a constant average and applied in total based on the quantity and volume of output—products made or services delivered. Of course, the actual expenses paid each accounting period to third parties and employees will always differ slightly from these averaged costs that were calculated "at standard," so there are various methods of cost variance analysis (e.g., volume variance, labor rate or price variance) to report what actually happened relative to what was planned and expected.

The overarching point here is that an organization's initial condition—the types of products and services it makes and delivers as well as its expense structure—governs its initial managerial accounting methodology.

AN ACCOUNTING FRAMEWORK AND TAXONOMY

There is a need for an overarching framework to describe how expenses are measured as costs and used in decision making. An understandable framework is not rocket science; it can be constructed and articulated. A framework created by Gary Cokins, one of this book's coauthors, for the International Federation of Accountants (www.ifac.org) is described here.

Exhibit 10.2 illustrates the large domain of accounting with three components: tax accounting, financial accounting, and managerial accounting. The exhibit is similar to taxonomies that biologists use to understand plant and animal kingdoms. A taxonomy defines the components that make up of a body of knowledge. In the figure there are two types of data sources displayed at the upper right. The upper source is from financial transactions and bookkeeping, such as purchases and payroll. The lower source is nonfinancial measures such as payroll hours worked, retail items sold, or gallons of liquid produced.

As mentioned earlier, the financial accounting component is intended for external reporting, such as for regulatory agencies, banks, stockholders, and the investment community. This information is mandatory. Financial accounting is governed by laws and rules established by regulatory agencies. In most nations, financial accounting follows generally accepted accounting principles (GAAP). Some people jokingly refer to this as the GAAP-trap because focusing on these numbers may distract the organization from more relevant accounting data or prevent it from finding more appropriate ways to calculate costs and profit margins. Financial accounting's purpose is for economic valuation, and as such is typically not adequate or sufficient for internal decision making.

The tax accounting component in Exhibit 10.2 has its own world of legislated rules.

Our area of concern is the managerial accounting component. It is used internally by managers and employee teams for insights and

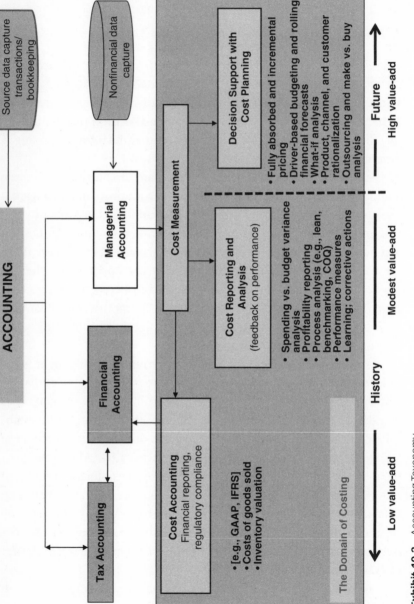

Exhibit 10.2 Accounting Taxonomy

The Domain of Costing

Cost Accounting
Financial reporting,
regulatory compliance

- [e.g., GAAP, IFRS]
- Costs of goods sold
- Inventory valuation

Cost Reporting and Analysis
(feedback on performance)

- Spending vs. budget variance analysis
- Profitability reporting
- Process analysis (e.g., lean, benchmarking, COQ)
- Performance measures
- Learning; corrective actions

Decision Support with Cost Planning

- Fully absorbed and incremental pricing
- Driver-based budgeting and rolling financial forecasts
- What-if analysis
- Product, channel, and customer rationalization
- Outsourcing and make vs. buy analysis

Cost Measurement

Managerial Accounting

Financial Accounting

Tax Accounting

ACCOUNTING

Source data capture transactions/ bookkeeping

Nonfinancial data capture

Low value-add ← History ← | → Future → High value-add

Modest value-add

foresight for better decision making. If you violate the financial accounting laws, you may go to jail. However, you don't risk going to jail if you have poor managerial accounting, but your organization runs the risk of making bad decisions. This is relevant because the margin for error is getting slimmer as the pressure grows for better organizational performance.

To oversimplify a distinction between financial and managerial accounting, financial accounting is about *valuation* and managerial accounting is about *value creation* through good decision making.

The managerial accounting component in Exhibit 10.2 is comprised of three parts that are all recipients of inputs from the "cost measurement" procedure of transforming incurred expenses (or their obligations) into calculated costs:

- *Cost accounting* represents the assignment of expenses into outputs, such as the cost of goods sold and the value of inventories. This box primarily provides external reporting to comply with regulatory agencies.

- *Cost reporting and analysis* represents the insights, inferences, and analysis of what has already taken place in the business—historical information—in order to understand and monitor performance.

- *Decision support with cost planning* involves decision making. It represents using the historical cost reporting information and its rates in combination with other economic information, including forecasts and planned changes (e.g., processes, products, services, channels) in order to test, validate, and make the types of decisions that lead to a financially successful and sustained future.

It will be apparent that the key differentiator between cost accounting and the other two uses of "cost measurement" is that cost accounting is deeply constrained by regulatory practices and describing the past in accordance with rules of financial accounting. The other two categories offer diagnostic support to interpret and draw inferences from what has already taken place and for what can happen in the future. Cost reporting and analysis are about explanation. Decision support with cost planning is about possibilities and probabilities.

WHAT? SO WHAT? THEN WHAT?

An important message at the bottom of Exhibit 10.2 is that the value, utility, and usefulness of the information increases, arguably at an exponential rate, moving from the left side to the right side of the diagram.

In Exhibit 10.2 the *cost accounting* data establishes a foundation; it is of low value for decision making. The *cost reporting and analysis* information converts cost measurement data into a context. It is useful for managers and employee teams to clearly observe outcomes with transparency that may have never been seen before, or that are dramatically different from their existing beliefs derived from their firm's less mature cost measurement method. Cost reporting displays the reality of what has happened, and provides answers to "What?" That is, for example, what did things cost last period?

However, an obvious follow-up question should be "So what?" That is, based on any questionable or bothersome observations, is there merit to making changes and interventions? How relevant to improving performance is the outcome we are seeing? But this leads to the more critical and relatively higher value-added need to propose actions—to make decisions—surfaced from *cost planning*. This is the "Then what?" question. For example, what change can be made or action taken (such as a distributor altering its truck and rail distribution routes), and what is the ultimate impact? Of course, changes will lead to multiple effects on service levels, quality, and delivery times, but the economic effect on profits and costs should also be considered. And this gets to the heart of the widening gap between accountants and decision makers who use accounting data. To close the gap, accountants must change their mind-set from managerial accounting to managerial economics—sometimes referred to as "decision-based costing."

There is a catch. When the *cost reporting and analysis* component shifts rightward to the *decision support with cost planning* box in Exhibit 10.2, then analysis shifts to the realm of decision support via economic analysis. For example, one needs to understand the impact that changes will have on future expenses. Therefore, the focus now shifts to resources and their capacities—which require expenses. This involves classifying the behavior of resource expenses as sunk, fixed, semifixed, variable, and so on, with changes in service offerings, volumes, mix, processes, and the like. This can be tricky. A key concept for these classifications is this: The "adjustability of capacity" of any individual resource expense depends on both the planning time horizon and the ease or difficulty of adjusting the individual resource's capacity (i.e., its stickability). This wanders into the messy area of marginal expense analysis that textbooks oversimplify, but is complicated to accurately calculate in the real world.

Exhibit 10.3 illustrates how a firm's view of its profit and expense structure changes as analysis shifts from the historical *cost reporting* view to a predictive *cost planning* view. The latter is the context from which decisions are considered and evaluated.

In the exhibit's left-hand side during the historical time period, the resource expenses were incurred. The capacities that incurred these expenses were supplied, and then they were either (1) *unused* as idle or protective capacity or (2) *used* to make products, to deliver customer services, or to internally sustain the organization. This is the *cost reporting and analysis* component from Exhibit 10.2 that calculates output costs. The money was spent, and costing answers where it was used. This is the descriptive view of costs. Accountants refer to this as full absorption costing when all the expenses for a past time period are totally traced to outputs. This approach traces expenses (and

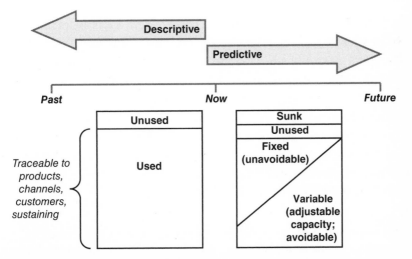

Exhibit 10.3 Descriptive versus Predictive Accounting

hopefully does not allocate expenses on causal-insensitive broad averages) to measure which outputs (e.g., products) uniquely consumed the resources. Full absorption costing uses direct costing methods, which are relatively easy to apply, and ideally supplements the reporting with activity-based costing techniques for the indirect and shared expenses—which are trickier to model, calculate, and report.

In contrast, Exhibit 10.3's right-hand side is the view of costs—the *decision support with cost planning* component from Exhibit 10.2. In the future, the capacity levels and types of resources can be adjusted. Capacity exists only as a resource, not as a process or work activity. The classification of an expense as sunk, fixed, semifixed, or variable depends on the planning time horizon. The diagonal line reveals that in the very short term, most expenses are not easily changed; hence, they are classified as fixed. As the time horizon extends into the future, then capacity becomes adjustable. For example, assets can be leased, not purchased; and future workers can be contracted from a temporary employment agency, not hired as full-time employees. Therefore, these expenses are classified as variable.

In the predictive view of Exhibit 10.3, changes in demand—such as the forecasted volume and mix of products and services ordered from customers—will drive the consumption of processes (and the work activities that belong to them). In turn, this will determine what level of both fixed and variable resource expenses are needed to supply capacity for future use. For purchased assets, such as retail store display shelves or expensive equipment, these costs are classified as sunk costs. Their full capacity and associated expense were acquired when an executive authorized and signed his or her name to the purchase order for the vendor or contractor. Some idle capacity (such as staffing a customer call center) is typically planned for. This deliberately planned idle capacity is intended to meet temporary demand surges, or as an insurance buffer for the uncertainty of the demand forecast accuracy. Its cost is justified by offsetting potential lost revenues from unacceptably low service levels to customers.

Since decisions only affect the future, the predictive view is the basis for analysis and evaluation. The predictive view applies techniques like what-if analysis and simulations. These projections are based on forecasts and consumption rates. However, consumption rates are ideally derived as calibrated rates from the historical, descriptive view—where the rate of operational work typically remains constant until productivity and process improvements affect it. These rates are for both direct expenses and rates that can be calibrated from an activity-based costing model for the indirect and shared expenses. And when improvements or process changes occur, the calibrated historical consumption rates can be adjusted up or down from the valid baseline measure that is already being experienced. Accountants refer to these projections as marginal expense analysis. For example, as future incremental demands change from the existing, near-term baseline operations, how is the supply for needed capacity affected?

COEXISTING COST ACCOUNTING METHODS

Confusion can arise because some costing methods calculate and report different costs that are not just variations in cost accuracy, but are also different reported costs altogether. This raises the question: "Should there be two or more different, *coexisting* cost reporting methods that report dissimilar numbers?" For example, one tactical costing method is used for operations (e.g., lean accounting) and making short-term decisions; another strategic costing method (for planning, marketing, pricing, and sales analysts to evaluate profit margins) is used for longer-term decisions.

There will be debates, but eventually some form of consensus will triumph within an organization. The underlying arguments may be due to the inappropriate usage of standard costing information—and potential inappropriate decisions and actions that may result. But there may be a deeper problem: Cost accounting system data is *not* the same thing as cost information that should be used for decision making. As described in Exhibit 10.3, the majority of value from cost information for decision making is not in historical reports—the descriptive view. Its primary value comes from planning the future (such as product and customer rationalization), marginal expense analysis for one-off decisions, or trade-off analysis between two or more alternatives.

The good news is that organizations are challenging traditional managerial accounting practices; so in the end, any accounting treatments that yield better decision making should prevail. The coexistence of two or more costing approaches may cause confusion over which one reports the correct cost. But that is a different problem. What matters is that organizations are seeking better ways to apply managerial accounting techniques to make better decisions.

PREDICTIVE ACCOUNTING WITH MARGINAL EXPENSE ANALYSIS[1]

Managers are increasingly shifting from reacting to after-the-fact outcomes to anticipating the future with predictive business analytics and proactively making adjustments with better decisions. Despite some advances in the application of new costing techniques, are management accountants adequately satisfying the need for better cost planning information? Or is the gap widening?

There is a widening gap between what management accountants report and what managers and employee teams want. This does not mean that information produced by management accountants is of little value. In the past few decades, accountants have made significant strides in improving the utility and accuracy of the historical costs they calculate and report. The gap is caused by a shift in managers' needs—from just needing to know what things cost (such as a product cost) and what happened to a need for reliable information about what their *future* costs will be and why.

Despite the accountants advancing a step to catch up with the increasing needs of managers to make good decisions, the managers have advanced two steps. In order to understand this widening gap, and more importantly how accountants can narrow and ideally close the gap, let us review the broad landscape of accounting as just described in the accounting taxonomy.

WHAT IS THE PURPOSE OF MANAGEMENT ACCOUNTING?

Contrary to beliefs that the only purpose of managerial accounting is to collect, transform, and report data, its primary purpose is first and foremost to influence behavior at all levels—from the desk of the CEO down to each employee—and it should do so by supporting decisions. A secondary purpose is to stimulate investigation and discovery by signaling relevant information (and consequently bringing focus) and generating questions.

The widening gap between what accountants report and what decision makers need involves the shift from analyzing *descriptive* historical information to analyzing *predictive* information, such as budgets and what-if scenarios. Obviously, all decisions can impact only the future because the past is already history. However, there is much that can be learned and leveraged from historical information. Although accountants are gradually improving the quality of reported history, decision makers are shifting their view toward better understanding the future.

This shift is a response to a more overarching shift in executive management styles—from a command-and-control emphasis that is reactive (such as scrutinizing cost variance analysis of actual versus planned outcomes) to an anticipatory, proactive style where organizational changes and adjustments, such as staffing levels, can be made before things happen and before minor problems become big ones.

WHAT TYPES OF DECISIONS ARE MADE WITH MANAGERIAL ACCOUNTING INFORMATION?

There are hundreds of pages on managerial and cost accounting in textbooks. We now try to distill all those pages to a few paragraphs. The broad decision-making categories for applying managerial accounting are:

- **Rationalization.** Which products, stock-keeping units (SKUs), services, channels, routes, customers, and so on are best to retain or improve? And which are not and should potentially be abandoned or terminated?

  Historical and descriptive costing (the left side of Exhibit 10.3) can be adequate to answer these questions. In part, this explains the growing popularity in applying activity-based costing principles to supplement traditional direct costing. There is much diversity and variation in routes, channels, customers, and so on that cause a relative increase in an organization's indirect and shared expenses to manage the resulting complexity. IT expenses are a growing example. Having the direct and indirect costs become a relevant starting point allows you to know what the variations cost. This answers the "What?" question. It is difficult, arguably impossible, to answer the subsequent "So what?" question without having the facts. Otherwise, conclusions are based on gut feel, intuition, misleading information, or politics.

■ **Planning and budgeting.** Based on forecasts of future demand volume and mix for types of services or products, combined with assumptions of other proposed changes, how much will it cost to match demand with supplied resources (e.g., workforce staffing levels)?

When questions like these and many more like them are asked, one needs more than a crystal ball to answer them. This is where the *predictive* view of costing (the right side of Exhibit 10.3) fits in. This is arguably the sweet spot of costing. On an annual cycle, this is the budgeting process. However, executives are increasingly demanding rolling financial forecasts at shorter intervals. This demand is partially due to the fact that the annual budget can quickly become obsolete, and future-period assumptions, especially continuously revised sales forecasts, become more certain. At its core, this costing sweet spot is about resource capacity planning (the ability to convert and reflect physical operational events into the language of money), expenses, and costs.

■ **Capital expense justification.** Is the return on investment (ROI) of a proposed asset purchase, such as equipment or an information system, justified?

If we purchase equipment, technology, or a system, will the financial benefits justify the investment? A question like this involves what microeconomics refers to as "capital budgeting." Capital budgeting analysis typically involves comparing a baseline, reflecting business as usual, with an alternative scenario that includes spending on (i.e., investing in) an asset where the expected benefits will continue well beyond a year's duration. An example would be investing in an automated warehouse to replace manual, pick-and-pack labor. Some refer to the associated investment justification analysis as "same as, except for" or comparing the as-is state with the to-be state. A distinction of capital budgeting is it involves discounted cash flow (DCF) equations. DCF equations reflect the net present value (NPV) of money, incorporating the time that it would take for that same money to earn income at some rate if it were applied elsewhere (e.g., a bank certificate of deposit). The rate is often called the organization's cost of capital.

- **Make-versus-buy and general outsourcing decisions.** Should we continue to do work ourselves or contract with a third party?

  If we choose to have a third party make our product or deliver our service instead of ourselves—basically outsourcing—or vice versa by bringing a supplier's work in-house, then afterward, how much of our expenses remain and how much will we remove (or add)? This type of decision is similar to the logic and math of capital budgeting. The same description of the capital budgeting method applies—measuring "same as, except for" incremental changes. Ideally, activity-based costing techniques should be applied because the primary variable is the work activities that the third-party contractor will now perform, which replace the current in-house work. Since cost is not the only variable that shifts, a service-level agreement with the contactor should be a standard practice.

- **Process and productivity improvement.** What can be changed? How to identify opportunities? How to compare and differentiate high-impact opportunities from nominal ones?

  Some organizations' operations functions are focusing on reducing costs and future cost avoidance. (Strategic profitable revenue enhancement is addressed with managerial accounting for *rationalization*.) These operational functions are tasked with productivity improvement challenges, and they are less interested in understanding strategic profitability analysis—which of our priced products and services makes or loses money—and more in streamlining processes, reducing waste and low-value-added work activities, and increasing asset utilization. This is the area of six sigma quality initiatives, lean management principles, and just-in-time (JIT) scheduling techniques. Examples of these types of costs are:

- Unit costs of outputs and benchmarking.
- Target costing.
- Cost of quality (COQ).
- Value-adding attributes (such as non-value-added vs. value-added).
- Resource consumption accounting (RCA).
- German cost accounting (*Grenzplankostenrechnung* [GPK]).
- Accounting for a lean management environment (also *kaizen* costing).
- Theory of constraint's throughput accounting.

The term *cost estimating* is a general one. It applies in all of these decision-making categories. One might conclude that the first category, rationalization, focuses only on historical costs and thus does not require cost estimates. However, the impact on resource expenses from adding or dropping various work-consuming outputs (i.e., products, services, customers) also requires cost estimates to validate the merits of a proposed rationalization decision.

ACTIVITY-BASED COST/MANAGEMENT AS A FOUNDATION FOR PREDICTIVE BUSINESS ACCOUNTING

In the late 1990s the more mature and advanced activity-based costing users increasingly began using their activity-based cost/management (ABC/M) calculated unit cost rates for intermediate work outputs and for products and services as a basis for estimating costs. As described earlier, popular uses of the activity-based costing data for cost estimating have been to calculate customer order quotations, to perform make-versus-buy analysis, and to budget. The ABC/M data was being recognized as a predictive planning tool. It is now apparent that the data has a tremendous amount of utility for both examining the as-is current condition of the organization and achieving a desired to-be state. (As mentioned earlier, a more robust version of ABC/M is called resource consumption accounting [RCA], based on the German accounting practice *Grenzplankostenrechnung* [GPK] for marginal expense analysis and flexible budgeting for operational control. RCA is a comprehensive approach that focuses on resources and capacity management logic with ABC/M principles.[2])

Cost estimating is often referred to as what-if scenarios. Regardless of what one calls the process, we are talking about the fact that decisions are being made about the future, and managers want to evaluate the consequences of those decisions. In these situations, the future is basically coming at the organization, and in some way the quantity and mix of activity drivers will be placing demands on the work that the organization will need to do. The resources required to do the work are the expenses. Assumptions are made about the outputs that are expected. Assumptions should also be made about the intermediate outputs and the labyrinth of interorganizational relationships that will be called upon to generate the expected final outcomes.

MAJOR CLUE: CAPACITY EXISTS ONLY AS A RESOURCE

As most organizations plan for their next month, quarter, or year, the level of resources supplied is routinely replanned to roughly match the firm's customer orders and expected future order demands. In reality, the level of planned resources must always exceed customer demand to allow for some protective buffer, surge, and sprint capacity. This also helps improve customer on-time shipping service performance levels. However, management accountants will be constantly disturbed if they cannot answer the question "How much unused and spare capacity do I have?" because in their minds this excess capacity equates to non-value-added costs.

The broad topic of unused and idle capacity will likely be a thorny issue for absorption costing. As management accountants better understand operations, they will be constantly improving their ability to segment and isolate the unused capacity (and the nature of its cost) by individual resource. Managerial accountants will be increasingly able to measure unused capacity either empirically or by deductive logic based on projected standard cost rates. Furthermore, accountants will be able to segment and assign this unused capacity expense to various processes, owners, the sales function, or senior management. This will eliminate overcharging (and overstating) product costs resulting from including unused capacity costs that the product did not cause.

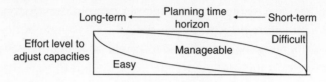

Exhibit 10.4   Capacity Exists Only as Resources

Exhibit 10.4 illustrates that the effort level to adjust capacity becomes easier farther out in time. It takes a while to convert in-case resources into as-needed ones. However, committed expenses (in-case) today can be more easily converted into contractual (as-needed) arrangements in a shorter time period than was possible 10 years ago.

For example, in the very short term, you would not fire employees on Tuesday due to a low work load but hire them back on Wednesday. But in the future you may replace full-time employees with contractors, or lease assets you might have purchased. In this way, so-called fixed costs behave variably.

Fixed expenses can become variable expenses. The rapid growth in the temporary staffing industry is evidence. Organizations are replacing full-time employees who are paid regardless of the demand level with contractors who are staffed and paid at the demand level, which may be measured in hours.

Understanding the cost of the resource workload used to make a product or to deliver a service is relevant to making these resource reallocation decisions. Ignoring incremental changes in the actual resources (i.e., expense spending) when making decisions can eventually lead to a cost structure that may become inefficient and ineffective for the organization. There will always be a need to adjust the capacity based on changes in future demand volume and mix. This in turn equates to raising or lowering specific expenses on resources.

PREDICTIVE ACCOUNTING INVOLVES MARGINAL EXPENSE CALCULATIONS

In forecasting, the demand volume and mix of the outputs are estimated, and one then solves for the unknown level of resource expenditures that will be required to produce and deliver the volume and mix. One is basically determining the capacity requirements of the resources. Estimating future levels of resource expense cash outflows becomes complex because resources come in discrete, discontinuous amounts. For example, you cannot hire one-third of an employee. That is, resource expenses do not immediately vary with each incremental increase or decrease in end-unit volume. Traditional accountants address this with what they refer to as a "step-fixed" category of expenses.

The predictive accounting method involves extrapolations that use baseline physical and cost consumption rates that are calibrated from prior-period ABC/M calculations. Managerial accountants relate predictive accounting to a form of flexible budgeting (which is normally applied annually to a 12-month time span).

Exhibit 10.5 illustrates how capacity planning is the key to the solution. Planners and budgeters initially focus on the direct and recurring resource expenses, not the indirect and overhead support expenses. They almost always begin with estimates of future demand in terms of volumes and mix. Then, by relying on standards and averages (such as the product routings and bills of material used in manufacturing systems), planners and budgeters calculate the future required levels of manpower and spending. The predictive accounting method suggests that this same approach can be applied to the indirect and overhead areas as well or to processes where the organization often has a wrong impression that it has no tangible outputs.

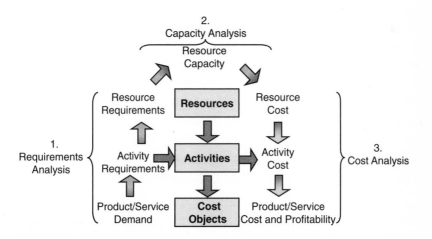

Exhibit 10.5 Predictive Accounting Information Flow

Demand volume drives activity and resource requirements. Predictive accounting is forward-focused, but it uses actual historical performance data to develop baseline consumption rates. Activity-based planning and budgeting assesses the quantities of workload demands that are ultimately placed on resources. In step 1 in Exhibit 10.5, predictive accounting first asks, "How much activity workload is required for *each* output of cost object?" These are the work activity requirements. Then predictive accounting asks, "How many resources are needed to meet that activity workload?" In other words, a workload can be measured as the number of units of an activity required to produce a quantity of cost objects.

The determination of expense does not occur until after the activity volume has been translated into resource capacity using the physical resource driver rates from the direct costing and ABC/M model. These rates are regularly expressed in hours, full-time equivalents (FTEs), square feet, pounds, gallons, and so forth.

As a result of step 1, there will be a difference between the existing resources available and the resources that will be required to satisfy the plan—the resource requirements. That is, at this stage organizations usually discover they may have too much of what they do not need and not enough of what they do need to meet the customers' expected service levels (e.g., to deliver on time). The consequence of having too much implies a cost of unused capacity. The consequence of having too little is a limiting constraint that if not addressed implies there will be a decline in customer service levels.

In step 2 a reasonable balance must be achieved between the operational and financial measures. Now capacity must be analyzed. One option is for the budgeters, planners, or management accountants to evaluate how much to adjust the shortage and excess of actual resources to respond to the future demand load. Senior management may or may not allow the changes. There is a maximum expense impact that near-term financial targets (and executive compensation plan bonuses) will tolerate. These capacity adjustments represent real resources with real changes in cash outlay expenses if they were to be enacted.

Assume that management agrees to the new level of resources without further analysis or debate. In step 3 of the flow in Exhibit 10.5, the new level of resource expenditures can be determined and then translated into the expenses of the work centers and eventually into the costs of the products, service lines, channels, and customers. Step 3 is classic cost accounting—but for a future period. Some call this a pro forma calculation. The quantities of the projected resource and activity drivers are applied, and new budgeted or planned costs can be calculated for products, service lines, outputs, customers, and service recipients.

At this point, however, the financial impact may not be acceptable. It may show too small a financial return. When the financial result is unacceptable, management has options other than to continue to keep readjusting resource capacity levels. For example, the company can limit customer orders accepted. These other options may not have much impact on expenses.

DECOMPOSING THE INFORMATION FLOWS FIGURE

Exhibit 10.6 decomposes Exhibit 10.5. It reveals five types of adjustments that planners and budgeters can consider to align their expected demand with resource expenditures to achieve desired financial results. This approach has been called a *closed-loop activity-based planning and budgeting (ABP/B)* framework.

Each of the five numbered options is intended to improve results; however, the relative impact of each adjustment will be unique to each organization and its situation. As previously described, the predictive accounting model uses as its source input the forecasted demand quantities to determine the degree of imbalance there may be between the required and the currently existing resources.

Assuming that the result will be shortages and excesses of capacity, management can make three operational changes:

1. **Adjust physical capacity.** Additional manpower, supplies, overtime, equipment, and the like can be purchased for shortages. There can be scale-backs and removals of people and machines for excesses.
2. **Adjust consumption rates.** If possible, the speed and efficiency of the existing resources can be cranked up or down.

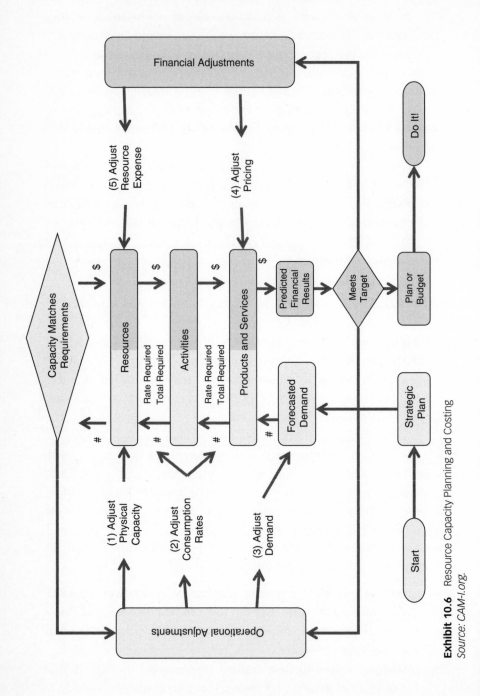

Exhibit 10.6 Resource Capacity Planning and Costing
Source: CAM-I.org.

If, for example, the increase in manpower makes a decision uneconomical, fewer people can be hired, with an assumed productivity rate increase.

3. **Adjust demand.** If resources remain constrained, demand can be governed or rationed.

The latter two options are operational but also affect the level of resource expenses required. After this cycle of adjustments balances capacity of supply with demand, if the financial results are still unsatisfactory, management can make two incremental financial changes:

4. **Adjust pricing.** In commercial for-profit enterprises or full cost recovery operations, pricing can be raised or lowered. This directly affects the top-line revenues. Of course, care is required because the price elasticity could cause changes in volume that more than offset the price changes.

5. **Adjust resource cost.** If possible, wage levels or purchase prices of materials can be renegotiated.

Predictive accounting acknowledges that there is a substantial amount of expenses that do not vary with a unit volume of final output. These expenses are not variable costs as determined by an incremental new expense for each incremental unit of output. As mentioned, resources often come in discontinuous amounts. Economists refer to these as step-fixed costs. An organization cannot purchase one-third of a machine or hire half an employee. Predictive accounting recognizes the step-fixed costs in step 2 of Exhibit 10.5 where resource capacity is adjusted. It recognizes that as external unit volumes fluctuate, then:

■ Some workload costs do eventually vary based on a batch size of output or on some other discretionary factor.

■ Some resource expenditures will be acquired or retired as a whole and indivisible resource, thus creating step-fixed expenses (i.e., adding or removing used and unused capacity expenses).

Absorption costing is descriptive; and the only economic property for costing you need to deal with is *traceability* of cost objects back to the resources they consume. However, the descriptive ABC/M data is used for predictive purposes. The data provides inferences. In contrast, predictive accounting is forward-looking. Predictive accounting strives to monitor the impact of decisions or plans in terms of the external cash funds flow of an organization. In the predictive view, determining the level of resource expenses gets trickier because you now have to consider an additional economic property—*variability*. The variability of resources is affected by two factors: (1) the step-fixed function since resources come in discontinuous amounts, and (2) adjustability of resources because the time delay to add or remove resource capacity can range from short to long.

Financial analysts simplistically classify costs as being either fixed or variable within the so-called relevant range of volume. In reality the classification of expenses as sunk, fixed, semifixed, semivariable, or variable depends on the decision being made. In the short term many expenses will not and cannot be changed. In the long term many of the expenses (e.g., capacity) can be adjusted.

FRAMEWORK TO COMPARE AND CONTRAST EXPENSE ESTIMATING METHODS

Exhibit 10.7 presents a framework that describes various methods of predictive cost estimating. The horizontal axis is the planning time horizon, short-term to long-term, right to left. The vertical axis describes the types and magnitudes of change in demands of the future relative to the recent past.

Examine the lower part of Exhibit 10.7, which illustrates the level of effort to adjust capacity across the planning time horizon. It describes expenses as becoming more variable and less committed as the planning time horizon lengthens. Historical cost rates can be more easily applied for longer time frame decisions; there are fewer step-fixed expense issues. There are no defined boundary lines between the various zones, and there is overlap as one estimating method gives way to another as being superior.

Exhibit 10.7 illustrates in the upper-right corner that as the time period to adjust capacity shortens and simultaneously the number of changes in conditions from the past substantially increases, it becomes risky to rely exclusively on rate-based extrapolation methods for cost

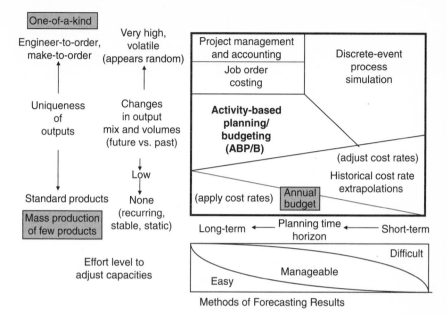

Exhibit 10.7 Expense Estimating Framework

forecasting. Discrete-event simulation tools may provide superior and more reliable answers in this zone relative to the other methods. Those tools can evaluate and validate decisions in any zone, but in particular in the upper-right corner of the exhibit.

PREDICTIVE COSTING IS MODELING

A commercial organization ultimately manages itself by understanding where it makes and loses money, or whether the impact of a decision produces incremental revenues superior to incremental expenses. Organizations are increasingly achieving a much better understanding of their contribution profit margins using ABC/M data. By leveraging ABC/M with predictive accounting and discrete event process simulation tools, an organization can produce a fully integrated plan, including budgets and rolling financial forecasts. It can be assured that its plan is more feasible, determine the level of resources and expenditures to execute that plan, and then view and compare the projected results of that plan against its current performance to manage its various profit margins.

The combination of these tools allows boardroom-level thinking to begin with the company's complete income statement, generate a feasible operating plan, and restate the results of that plan with an income statement—again for boardroom reporting. Advocates of simulation planning software believe that the brute-force computing power of personal computers and/or seamless integration with servers now adequately provides simulation information that is comprehensive, finite-scheduled, and rule-based and allows for various assumptions about uncertainty. Others argue that this is a last resort, and that good modeling provides sufficiently accurate results.

All this may seem like revisiting an introductory economics textbook. In some ways it is, but here is the difference: In the textbooks, marginal expense analysis was something easily described but extremely difficult to compute due to all of the complexities and interdependencies of resources and their costs. In the past, computing technology was the impediment. Now things have reversed. Technology is no longer the impediment—the thinking is. How one configures the predictive accounting model, and what assumptions one makes, becomes critical to calculating the appropriate required expenses and their pro forma calculated costs.

DEBATES ABOUT COSTING METHODS

Confusion can arise because some of the costing methods calculate and report different costs that are not just variations in cost accuracy, but are also different cost amounts. For example, should there be two or more different, *coexisting* cost reporting methods that report dissimilar numbers? One tactical costing method might be used for operations and making short-term decisions; another strategic costing method (for planning, marketing, pricing, and sales analysts to evaluate profit margins) is used for longer-term decisions.

There will be debates, but eventually some form of consensus will triumph within an organization. The underlying arguments may be due to the inappropriate usage of standard costing information—and the potential inappropriate actions that may result. Therefore, key tests for deciding which costing method to use should be: How does it handle economic projections? Can it accommodate classifying resource expenses as variable, semivariable, semifixed, fixed, sunk, or as unavoidable or avoidable (i.e., allowing for capacity adjustment decisions)? Does it isolate unused/idle capacity expenses?

The good news is that organizations are challenging traditional accounting; so in the end, any accounting treatments that yield better decision making should prevail. The coexistence of two or more costing approaches may cause confusion over which one reports the correct cost. But that is a different problem. What matters is that organizations are seeking better ways to apply managerial accounting techniques to make better decisions.

SUMMARY

What we have learned in this chapter is that when managerial accounting shifts from historical costing of what happened to the projected view of what can happen, then techniques involve managerial economics. That is, for the predictive view the behavior of the resource capacity expenses relative to changes in demands must be classified as sunk, fixed, semifixed (step), semivariable, variable, or discretionary.

What we also have learned is that in order to model and calculate the projected expenses, the unit-level cost consumption rates must be derived from an effective historical costing system. So historical costing is a prerequisite for predictive accounting.

Finally, we have learned that there can be two or more coexisting costing methods for a same organization. They will serve different purposes. One may be for strategic decisions and another for process and cost management productivity improvement purposes.

NOTES

1. The ideas in this chapter on activity-based resource planning (ABRP) are based on the research from the Activity Based Budgeting Project Team of the Consortium of Advanced Manufacturing—International's (CAM-I) Cost Management Systems (CMS) group. More is at www.cam-i.org.
2. More can be learned about RCA at www.rcainfo.com.

CHAPTER 11

Driver-Based Budget and Rolling Forecasts

Prediction is very difficult, especially about the future.

—Niels Bohr

Recently, there has been an active, sometimes emotional discussion regarding the value of the annual budgeting process. Though we would like to weigh in on this discussion (and have in past in other venues), it seems appropriate that in this chapter we focus on budgeting and forecasting as these applications are related to predictive business analytics.

Make your own judgment by answering these questions: (1) How many people in your organization love the annual budgeting process? Probably none. (2) Does the mere mention of the word *budget* raise eyebrows and evoke cynicism? It should. (3) As a simple test, how many boxes in Exhibit 11.1 would be checked as applicable to your organization? Probably all.

What is broken about the annual budgeting process? We can more deeply discuss some of the issues related to budgeting:

- **Obsolete budgeting.** The budget data is obsolete within weeks after it is published because of ongoing changes in the

    ☐ is invasive and time-consuming, with few benefits.

    ☐ takes 14 months from start to end.

    ☐ requires two or more executive tweaks at the end.

    ☐ is obsolete in two months due to events and reorganizations.

    ☐ starves the departments with truly valid needs.

    ☐ caves in to the loudest voice and political muscle.

    ☐ rewards veteran sandbaggers who are experts at padding.

    ☐ incorporates last year's inefficiencies into this year's budget.

    ☐ Is overstated from the prior year's "use it or lose it" spending.

Exhibit 11.1   A Quiz: "Our Annual Budgeting Exercise…"

environment. Customers and competitors usually change their behavior after the budget is published, and a prudent reaction to these changes often cannot be accommodated in the budget. In addition, today's budget process takes an extraordinarily long time, sometimes exceeding a year, during which the organization often reshuffles and resizes.

- **Bean-counter budgeting.** The budget is considered a fiscal exercise produced by the accountants and is disconnected from the strategy of the executive team—and from the mission-critical spending needed to implement the strategy. In addition, it is often not volume sensitive with changes in work activity drivers.

- **Political budgeting.** The loudest voice, the greatest political muscle, and the prior year's budget levels should not be valid ways to award resources for next year's spending.

- **Overscrutinized budgeting.** Often the budget is revised midyear or, more frequently, with new forecast spending. Then an excess amount of attention focuses on analyzing the differences between the actual and projected expenses. These include budget-to-forecast, last-forecast-to-current-forecast, actual-to-budget, actual-to-forecast, and so on. This reporting provides lifetime job security for the budget analysts in the accounting department.

- **Sandbagging budgeting.** The budget numbers that roll up from lower-level and midlevel managers often mislead senior executives because of sandbagging (i.e., padding) by the veteran managers who know how to play the game.

- **Wasteful budgeting.** Budgets do not identify waste. In fact, inefficiencies in the current business processes are often baked into next year's budget. Budgets do not support continuous improvement.

- **Blow-it-all budgeting.** Reckless "use it or lose it" spending is standard practice for managers during the last fiscal quarter who realize they are not on track to spend their full year's approved budget. They view its approval from a year earlier as an authorization to spend because "It's in my budget!" Budgets can be an invitation to managers to spend needlessly.

- **Spreadsheet budgeting.** There is excessive use of offline spreadsheets for different departments and cost centers. Each spreadsheet is typically inconsistent with the others. There are all sorts of data governance and control issues, especially for managers who want to change the spreadsheet equations and formats. Consolidating them into a unified budget can be a nightmare.

The annual budget is steeped in tradition, yet the effort of producing it heavily outweighs the benefits it supposedly yields. The budget is typically not tightly linked with the executive team's strategy. In most organizations there is a grand and overly vague long-term mission described from the top and detailed multiyear plans with a short-term budget at the bottom. The problem is there nothing in between to link the two together! With today's volatile world, the long term does not start in the fifth year of the current five-year plan. It starts right now!

Another problem with the annual budgeting process is it is typically derived from the bottom up from excessive general-ledger cost-center expense line-item detail. Cost modeling of the annual budget is a superior top-down method relying of forecasts of a few key independent variables from which dependent expense variables can be calculated.

How can budgeting be reformed and streamlined? Or should the budget process be abandoned altogether because its inflexible fixed "social contract" incentives to managers drive behavior counter to the organization's changing goals and its unwritten "earnings contract" with shareholders? And, if the budget is abandoned, then what should replace its underlying purpose?

EVOLUTIONARY HISTORY OF BUDGETS

Why were budgets invented? Organizations seem to go through an irreversible life cycle that leads them toward specialization and eventually to turf protection. When organizations are originally created, managing spending is fairly straightforward. With the passing of time, the number and variety of their products and service lines change as well as the needs of their customers. This introduces complexity and results in more indirect expenses and overhead to manage the newly created complexity.

Following an organization's initial creation, all of the workers are reasonably focused on fulfilling the needs of whatever created the organization in the first place. Despite early attempts to maintain flexibility, organizations slowly evolve into separate functions. As the functions create their own identities and staff, they seem to become fortresses. In many of them, the work becomes the jealously guarded property of the occupants. Inside each fortress, allegiances grow, and people speak their own languages—an effective way to spot intruders and confuse communications.

With the passing of more time, organizations then become internally hierarchical. This structure exists even though the transactions and work flows that provide value and service to the ultimate customers pass through and across internal and artificial organizational boundaries. These now-accepted management hierarchies are often referred to, within the organization itself as well as in management literature, as "silos," "stovepipes," or "smokestacks." The structure causes managers to act in a self-serving way, placing their functional needs above those of the cross-functional processes to which each function contributes. In effect, the managers place their personal needs above the needs of their coworkers and customers.

At this stage in its life, the organization becomes less sensitive to the sources of demand placed on it from the outside and to changes in customer needs. In other words, the organization begins to lose sight of its raison d'être. The functional silos compete for resources and blame one another for any of the organization's inexplicable and continuing failures to meet the needs of its customers. Arguments emerge about the source of the organization's inefficiencies, but they are difficult to explain.

The accountants do not help matters. They equate the functional silos to the responsibility cost center view that they capture expense transactions in their general-ledger accounting system. When they request each cost center manager to submit the next year's budget, ultimately it is an "incremental or decremental" game. That is, each manager begins with his or her best estimate of the current year's expected total spending—line item by line item—and incrementally increases it with a percentage. Budgeting software reinforces this bad habit by making it easy to make these calculations. At the very extreme, next year's spending for each line is computed as shown in Exhibit 11.2. Using spreadsheet software, you multiply the first line-item expense by the increment, in this example by 5 percent, and simply copy and paste that formula for every line item below it. Isn't it laughable? But the truth hurts. This is what leads to the use-it-or-lose-it unnecessary blow-it-all spending described earlier.

By this evolution point in budgeting, there is poor end-to-end visibility about what exactly drives what inside the organization. Some organizations eventually evolve into intransigent bureaucracies. Some functions become so embedded inside the broader organization that their work level is insensitive to changes in the number and types of external requests. Fulfilling these requests was the origin of why the functions were created in the first place. They become insulated from the outside world. This is not a pleasant story, but it is pervasive.

	Current Year	Budget Year
Wages	$ 400,000.00	Formula = Column b * 1.05
Supplies	$ 50,000.00	
Rent	$ 20,000.00	Copy down
Computer	$ 40,000.00	
Travel	$ 30,000.00	
Phone	$ 20,000.00	
Total	$ 560,000.00	

Exhibit 11.2 Spreadsheet Budgeting—It Is Incremental

A SEA CHANGE IN ACCOUNTING AND FINANCE

How can budgeting be reformed? Let us step back and ask broader questions. What are the impacts of the changing role of the chief financial officer (CFO)? How many times have you seen the obligatory diagram with the organization shown in a central circle and a dozen inward-pointing arrows representing the menacing forces and pressures the organization faces—such as outsourcing, globalization, governance, brand preservation, and so on? Well, it is all true and real. But if the CFO's function is evolving from a bean counter and reporter of history into a strategic business adviser and an enterprise risk and regulatory compliance manager, what are CFOs doing about the archaic budget process?

Progressive CFOs now view budgeting as consisting of three streams of spending that converge as a river:

1. **Recurring expenses.** Budgeting becomes an ongoing resource capacity planning exercise similar to a 1970s factory manager who must project the operation's manpower planning and material purchasing requirements.

2. **Nonrecurring expenses.** The budget includes the one-time investments or project cash outlays to implement strategic initiatives.

3. **Discretionary expenses.** The budget includes optional spending that is nonstrategic.

Of the broad portfolio of interdependent methodologies that make up today's enterprise performance management (EPM) framework, two methods deliver the capability to accurately project the recurring and nonrecurring spending streams:

1. **Activity-based planning.** In the 1990s, activity-based costing (ABC) solved the structural deficiencies of myopic general-ledger cost-center reporting for calculating accurate costs of outputs (such as products, channels, and customers). The general ledger does not recognize cross-functional business processes that deliver the results, and its broad-brush cost allocations of the now-substantial indirect expenses introduce grotesque cost

distortions. ABC corrects those deficiencies. Advances to ABC's historical snapshot view transformed it into activity-based management (ABM). These advances project forecasts of customer demand item volume and mix and forecast the elusive customer cost-to-serve requirements. In effect, ABC is calculated backward, and named activity-based planning, based on ABC's calibrated consumption rates to determine the needed capacity and thus the needed recurring expenses. Without that spending, service levels will deteriorate.

2. **Balanced scorecard and strategy maps.** By communicating the executive strategy and involving managers and employee teams to identify the projects and initiatives required to achieve the strategy map's objectives, nonrecurring expenses are funded. Without that spending, managers will be unjustly flagged red as failing to achieve the key performance indicators (KPIs) they are responsible for in their balanced scorecards.

FINANCIAL MANAGEMENT INTEGRATED INFORMATION DELIVERY PORTAL

Today's solution to solve the budgeting conundrum and the organization's backward-looking focus is to begin with a single integrated data platform—popularly called a business intelligence platform—and its web-based reporting and analysis capabilities. Speed to knowledge is now a competitive differentiator.

The emphasis for improving an organization and driving higher value must shift from hand-slap controlling toward automated forward-looking planning. With a common platform replacing disparate data sources, enhanced with input data integrity cleansing features and data mining capabilities, an organization can create a flexible and collaborative planning environment. It can provide on-demand information access to all for what-if scenario and trade-off analysis. For the bold CFO who is not wary of radical change, continuous and valid rolling financial forecasts can replace the rigid annual budget. Organizations need to be able to answer more questions than "Are we going to hit our numbers in December?" That's not planning but rather performance evaluation. For the traditional CFO, the integrated data platform offers a sorely needed high-speed budgeting process.

In addition, statistical forecasting can be combined with the integrated information on the platform, resulting in customer demand forecasting that seamlessly links to operational systems, activity-based planning, and balanced scorecard initiatives for the ultimate financial view the CFO can now offer to his or her managers. Real-time or right-time feedback to managers is part of the package.

All of this—traffic-signaling dashboards, profitability reporting and analysis, consolidation reporting, dynamic drill-down, customizable exception alert messaging to minimize surprises, Excel linkages, multiple versioning, and more—is available for decision making on a single shared solution architecture platform. EPM resolves major problems: lack of visibility to causality, lack of timely and reliable information, poor understanding of the executive team's strategy, and wasted resources due to misaligned work processes.

Some organizations have become sufficiently frustrated with the annual budgeting process that they have abandoned creating a budget. An international research and membership collaborative called the Beyond Budgeting Round Table (BBRT)[1] advocates that rather than attempt to tightly control spending on a line-by-line basis, it is better to step back and question what the purposes of budgeting are. The BBRT's conclusion is that organizations would be better off moving away from long-term financial projections at a detailed level and replace this form of monitoring by empowering managers with more freedom to make local spending decisions, including hiring employees.

BBRT believes in removing second-guess approvals from higher-level managers and granting managers more decision rights. BBRT views fiscal year-end budget figures as if they are a fixed contract that managers will strive for rather than react to changes not assumed when the budget was created. In place of budget spending variance controls, BBRT advocates a shift in reporting emphasis and also accountability with consequences on outcomes—performance reporting—not on the inputs. BBRT believes that secondary purposes for budgeting, such as cash flow projections for the treasury function, can be attained with modeling techniques performed by analysts. These modeling techniques are a major reason for reliable forecasts and a sound managerial accounting system to calibrate currently experienced consumption rates.

Regardless of how an organization approaches its own reforms to budgeting, EPM provides confidence in the numbers, which improves trust among managers. What today will accelerate the adoption of reforms to the budgeting process and an EPM culture—senior management's attitude and willpower or the information technology that can realize the vision described here? We would choose both.

PUT YOUR MONEY WHERE YOUR STRATEGY IS

Two easy ways for executive teams to attempt to raise profits is to lay off employees to cut costs or to lower prices to take away market share from their competitors. But these are merely short-term fixes. An organization cannot continue to endlessly reduce its costs and prices to achieve long-term sustained prosperity.

Entrepreneurs know the age-old adage that "you need to spend money to make money." However, belt-tightening an organization's spending can be haphazard. Rather than evaluating where the company can cut costs, it is more prudent to switch views and ask where and how the organization should spend money to increase long-term sustained value. This involves budgeting for future expenses, but the budgeting process has deficiencies.

PROBLEM WITH BUDGETING

Companies cannot succeed by standing still. If you are not improving, then others will soon catch up to you. This is one reason why Professor Michael E. Porter, author of the seminal 1980 book on competitive edge strategies, *Competitive Strategy: Techniques for Analyzing Industries and Competitors*,[2] asserts that an important strategic approach is continuous differentiation of products and services to enable premium pricing. However, some organizations have believed so firmly in their past successes that they have gone bankrupt because they had become risk-adverse to changing what they perceived to be effective strategies.

Strategy execution is considered one of the major failures of executive teams. At a 2006 conference, Dr. David Norton, coauthor with

Professor Robert S. Kaplan of *The Balanced Scorecard: Translating Strategy into Action*,[3] stated, "Nine out of 10 organizations fail to successfully implement their strategy. . . . The problem is not that organizations don't manage their strategy well; it is they do not formally manage their strategy."[4] Empirical evidence confirms that companies execute strategy poorly. Involuntary turnover of North American CEOs in 2006 likely beat the record high set just the previous year.[5] In defense of executives, they often formulate good strategies—their problem is failure to execute them.

One of the obstacles preventing successful strategy achievement is the annual budgeting process. In the worst situations, the budgeting process is limited to a fiscal exercise administered by the accountants, who are typically disconnected from the executive team's strategic intentions. A less poor situation, but still not a solution, is one in which the accountants do consider the executive team's strategic objectives, but the initiatives required to achieve the strategy are not adequately funded in the budget. Remember, you have to spend money to make money.

In addition, the budgeting process tends to be insensitive to changes in future volumes and mix of forecast products and services. As described in the prior chapter, the next year's budgeted spending is typically incremented or decremented for each cost center from the prior year's spending by a few percentage points.

Components of the EPM framework can be drawn on to resolve these limitations. Exhibit 11.3 illustrates in the big arrow at the right

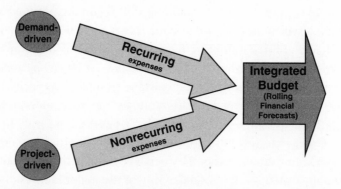

Exhibit 11.3 Resource Requirements Are Derived

side that the correct and valid amount of spending for capacity and consumed expenses should be derived from two broad streams of workload that cause the need for spending—demand driven and project driven. Demand-driven expenses are operational and recurring from day to day. In contrast, project-driven spending is nonrecurring and can be from days to years in time duration.

VALUE IS CREATED FROM PROJECTS AND INITIATIVES, NOT THE STRATEGIC OBJECTIVES

A popular solution for failed strategy execution is the evolving methodology of a strategy map with its companion, the balanced scorecard. Their combined purpose is to link operations to strategy. By using these methodologies, alignment of the work and priorities of employees can be attained without any disruption from restructuring the organizational chart. The balanced scorecard directly connects the executive team's strategy to individuals, regardless of their departments or matrix-management arrangements.

Although many organizations claim to use dashboards and performance scorecards, there is little consensus on how to design or apply these tools. At best, the balanced scorecard has achieved a brand status but without prescribed rules on how to construct or use it. For example, many companies claim to have a balanced scorecard, but it may have been developed in the absence of a strategy map from executives. Some companies design scorecards and perceive that if they use four dimensions, then they have achieved a balanced scorecard. This is like buying a set of golf clubs, a dozen golf balls, and a stylish pair of slacks and believing they can play golf.

The strategy map is arguably many orders of magnitude more important than the balanced scorecard. Therefore, when organizations simply display their so-called scorecard of actual versus planned or targeted metrics on a dashboard, how do the users know that the KPIs displayed in the dials reflect the strategic intent of their executives? They may not! At a basic level, the balanced scorecard is simply a feedback mechanism to inform users how they are performing on preselected measures that are ideally causally linked. To improve, much more information than just reporting your score is needed.

One source of confusion in the strategy management process involves misunderstandings of the role of projects and initiatives. For the minority of companies that realize the importance of first developing their strategy maps before jumping ahead to designing their balanced scorecards, there is another methodology challenge. Should organizations first select and set the targets for the scorecard KPIs, and subsequently determine the specific projects and initiatives that will help reach those targets? Or should the sequence be reversed? Should organizations first propose the projects and initiatives based on the strategy map's various theme objectives, and then derive the KPIs with their target measures afterward?

We could debate the proper order and argue that projects and initiatives should be defined from the strategy map. Putting this argument aside, what matters more is that the projects and initiatives be financially funded regardless of how they are identified.

In Exhibit 11.4, the second column of "X" choices, what if the managers and employee teams that identified the projects are not granted spending approval by the executives for those initiatives? Presuming that KPIs with targets were established for those projects, these managers will score poorly and unfavorably. But worse yet, the strategic objectives the projects are intended to achieve will not be accomplished. By isolating this spending as strategy expenses, the organization protects these; otherwise it is like destroying the seeds for future success and growth. Capital budgeting is a more mature practice and not the issue that budgeting for strategic projects and initiatives is.

Measurement Period	1st Quarter					
	Strategic Objective	Identify Projects, Initiatives, or Processes	KPI Measure	KPI Target	KPI Actual	Comments/ Explanation
Executive Team	X			X		
Managers and Employees		X	X		Their score	X
					<----- Period results ------->	

Exhibit 11.4 Nonrecurring Expenses/Strategic Initiatives

Value creation does not directly come from defining mission, vision, and strategy maps. It is the alignment of employees' priorities, work, projects, and initiatives with the executive team's objectives that directly creates value. Strategy is executed from the bottom to the top. Dr. Norton uses a fishermen's analogy to explain this: Strategy maps tell you where the fish are, but it is the projects, initiatives, and core business processes that catch the fish.

DRIVER-BASED RESOURCE CAPACITY AND SPENDING PLANNING

For daily operations where the normal recurring work within business processes occurs, a future period's amount of product-line and service-line volume and mix will never be identical to the past. In future periods, some customer-demand quantities will rise and others decline. This means that unless the existing capacity and dedicated skills are adjusted, you will have too much unnecessary capacity and not enough capacity that is needed. These are dual problems. The former results in unused capacity expenses. The latter results in missed sales opportunities, or customer-infuriating delays due to capacity shortages. Both drag down profits.

Exhibit 11.5 illustrates advances in applying activity-based cost/ management (ABC/M) to minimize this planning problem. ABC/M principles solve operational budgeting by leveraging historical

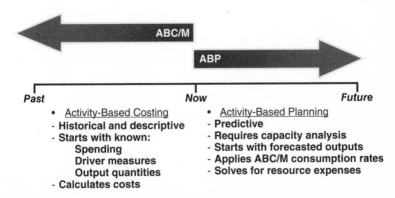

Exhibit 11.5 Recurring Expenses/Future Volume and Mix

consumption rates to be used for calculating future-period levels of capacity and spending.

As an oversimplification, future spending is derived by calculating the ABC/M cost assignment network backward. This was described in Chapter 10 as closed-loop activity-based planning and budgeting (ABP/B). The organization starts by forecasting its activity-driver quantities (those were the actual driver quantities for past-period costing). Then, it uses the calibrated activity driver unit-level consumption rates from its historical costing to compute the amount of required work activities in the operational processes. Next, it equates these workloads into the number and types of employees and the needed non-labor-related spending.

This technique provides the correct, valid capacity and spending requirements. With this knowledge, management can intelligently intervene and approve adjustments by adding or removing capacity. It is a logical way of matching supply with demand. Once the capacity interventions (e.g., employee head count) and planned spending are approved, then a true and valid driver-based budget can be derived—not an incremental or decremental percentage change from last year—for each cost center.

INCLUDING RISK MITIGATION WITH A RISK ASSESSMENT GRID

Measuring and managing risk possibilities is now transitioning from an intuitive art to more of a craft and a science. To introduce quantification to this area that involves qualitative and subjectivity, at some stage each identified risk requires some form of ranking, such as by level of importance—high, medium, and low. Since the importance of a risk event includes not just its impact but also its probability of occurrence, developing a risk assessment grid can be a superior method to quantify the risks and then collectively associate and rationalize all of them with a reasoned level of spending for risk mitigation. A risk map helps an organization visualize all risks on a single page.

Exhibit 11.6 displays a risk assessment grid with the vertical axis reflecting the magnitude of impact of the risk event occurring on the strategy execution and the horizontal axis reflecting the probability

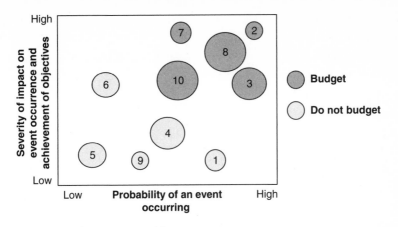

Exhibit 11.6 Risk Assessment Grid

of each risk event's occurrence. Individual risk events located in the map are inherent risks and not yet selected for mitigation actions; that evaluation comes next. The risks located in the lower-left area require periodic glances to monitor if the risk is growing; they require nominal to no risk mitigation spending. At the other extreme, risk events in the upper-right area deserve risk mitigation spending with frequent monitoring.

The risks in the risk assessment grid are evaluated for mitigation action. What this grid reveals is that risks number 2, 3, 7, 8, and 10 are in a critical zone. Management must decide if it can accept these five risks considering their potential impact and likelihood. If not, management might choose to avoid whatever is creating the risk as, for example, entering a new market. Some mitigation action might be considered that would drive the risks to a more acceptable level in terms of impact and likelihood. As examples, an action might result in transferring some of the risk through a joint venture; or it might involve incurring additional expense through hedging.

Management must decide on the cost versus benefits of the mitigation actions. Will a mitigation action, if pursued, move a risk event within the predefined risk appetite guidelines? Is the residual risk remaining after mitigation action acceptable? If not, what additional action can be taken? How much will that additional action cost, and what will be the potential benefits in terms of reducing impact and likelihood? After these decisions are made, then similar to the projects and initiatives derived from the strategy map, risk mitigation actions can be budgeted.

FOUR TYPES OF BUDGET SPENDING: OPERATIONAL, CAPITAL, STRATEGIC, AND RISK

Exhibit 11.7 illustrates a broad framework that begins with strategy formulation at left and ends with financial budgeting and rolling forecasts at right. The elements involving accounting are shaded. Some budgets and rolling financial forecasts may distinguish the capital budget spending from operational budget spending, but rarely do organizations segregate the important strategic budget spending and risk budget spending.

The main purpose of the exhibit is to illustrate that the budget depends on and is derived from two separate sources: (1) a future demand-driven source (operational) and (2) a project-based source (capital, strategic, and risk mitigation).

Ideally, the strategy creation at left uses meaningful managerial accounting information, such as understanding which products and customers are more or less profitable today and will be potentially more valuable in the future. With this additional knowledge, the executives can determine which strategic objectives to focus on.

Note that the operational budget, those expenses required to continue with day-to-day repeatable processes, is calculated based on forecasted volume and mix of drivers of processes, such as the sales forecast, multiplied by planned consumption rates that are calibrated from past time periods (and ideally with rates reflecting planned productivity gains). This demand-driven method contrasts with the too-often primitive budgeting method of simply increasing the prior year's spending level by a few percentage points to allow for inflation. The operational budget spending level is a dependent variable based on demand, so it should be calculated that way.

Regardless of whether an organization defines the strategic initiatives before or after setting the balanced scorecard's KPI targets, it is important to set aside strategy spending not much differently than budgeting for capital expenditures. Too often, the strategy funding is

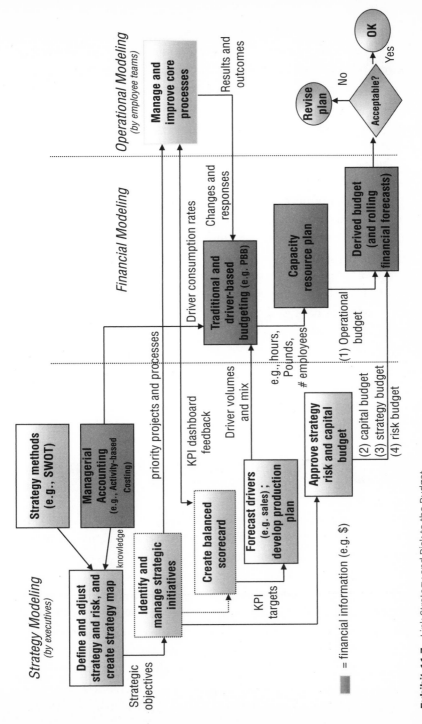

Exhibit 11.7 Link Strategy and Risk to the Budget

Source: Analytics-Based Performance Management LLC, www.garycokins.com, copyright 2013.

not cleanly segregated anywhere in the budget or rolling financial forecasts. It is typically buried in an accounting ledger expense account. As a result, when financial performance inevitably falls short of expectations, it is the strategy projects' seed money that gets deferred or eliminated. This priority must be reversed. Organizations must protect strategy spending and allow it to go forward, as it is the key to competitive differentiation and successfully accomplishing the strategy.

The same goes for the risk mitigation expenses. Enterprise risk management should be included in spending projections.

Note the question "Acceptable?" in the diamond located in the bottom right corner of Exhibit 11.7. Since the first pass at the derived budget or rolling forecast will likely be unacceptably high and rejected by the executive team, the result is to adjust the plan. Hopefully, the project-based, strategy budget spending will be protected. As previously mentioned, organizations must protect strategy spending and allow it to go forward because it is a key to competitive differentiation and successfully accomplishing the strategy, similarly with the risk mitigation spending. Once the strategy and risk management spending are protected, the only other lever is to plan for productivity improvements in the consumption rates. It is in this way that focused cost reductions (or future cost avoidance) become part of the EPM framework.

Put your money where your strategy is!

FROM A STATIC ANNUAL BUDGET TO ROLLING FINANCIAL FORECASTS

Most executive teams request frequent updates and revisions of the financial budget. These are referred to as rolling financial forecasts because the projection's planning horizon is usually well beyond the fiscal year-end date, such as out 18 months to two years.

Rolling forecasts are a more fluid approach to planning. Their use may even lead to abandoning a typical annual plan, especially where there is much volatility and uncertainty. They recognize the constant forward movement of any business. It is a continuous process and a more proactive approach that is synchronized with the business.

Imagine if you're a chief financial officer or financial controller required to reprocess the budget as a rolling forecast quarterly (or even monthly). There are not enough spreadsheets to do it! Only with computer automation that integrates several of the methodologies of the EPM framework, including good predictive analytics, can an organization produce valid derived rolling financial forecasts.

Rolling financial forecasts require less administrative effort once they are implemented. They mainly require forecasts of key independent variables from which other expense levels are calculated. This reduces the cost of doing business and results in less burnout of those mired in the traditional budgeting process. More important, it frees up available time for other higher-valued activities, including analysis.

MANAGING STRATEGY IS LEARNABLE

Organizations with a formal strategy execution process dramatically outperform organizations without formal processes. Building a core competency in strategy execution creates a competitive advantage for commercial organizations and increases value for constituents of public-sector organizations. Managing strategy is learnable. It is important to include and protect planned spending for strategic projects and initiatives in budgets and rolling financial forecasts. Those projects lead to long-term sustainable value creation.

SUMMARY

We have learned in this chapter that there is controversy about the annual budgeting process. There are questions related to whether its benefits are worth the effort and whether it might be obsolete in a few months after being officially published. More critical questions involve the traditional method of slightly incrementing or decrementing each cost center's expenses using the prior year as a baseline to reflect inflation or wage increases without applying cost consumption rates derived at a unit level of volume demand placed on the work activities in each cost center. Other concerns are that the budget is not sufficiently linked to the strategy and to the projects and initiatives that are needed to execute the strategy.

We have learned that a method to replace the traditional budget reflects the two main drivers that the appropriate level of resource capacity expenses: (1) recurring expenses that are demand driven, and (2) nonrecurring expenses that are project driven. The former relies on multiplying calibrated cost consumption rates by forecasted volume of outputs. The latter is comprised of three types of projects: (1) strategic projects derived from the strategic objectives in a strategy map, (2) risk-mitigation projects derived from a systematic enterprise risk management (ERM) program, and (3) capital investment projects.

We further learned that to typically adjust downward the final spending levels to satisfy expectations of the executives and investors, rather than postpone or eliminate the three types of projects that would jeopardize longer-term performance, the prudent adjustment should be to achieve productivity improvements in the business processes. Achieve the same level of outputs with lower resource expenses.

Finally, we learned that if the managerial accounting system is sufficiently automated and forecasts can be updated at regular intervals, say quarterly or monthly; then rolling financial forecasts based on modeling and the interdependent relations in the model can replace the annual budget.

NOTES

1. BBRT – Beyond Budgeting Roundtable, www.bbrt.org.
2. Michael E. Porter, *Competitive Strategy: Techniques for Analyzing Industries and Competitors* (New York: Free Press, 1980).
3. David Norton and Robert S. Kaplan, *The Balanced Scorecard: Translating Strategy into Action* (Boston: Harvard Business Review Press, 1996).
4. Dr. David Norton, Balanced Scorecard Collaborative Summit, San Diego, California, November 7, 2006.
5. Del Jones, "Turnover for CEOs Is on Record Pace," *USA Today*, July 12, 2006, 2B.

PART FIVE

Trends and Organizational Challenges

CHAPTER **12**

CFO Trends

At the end of the day (referring to management reports),
I am either happy or sad; what is important is to know why.

—Warren Jenson, former CFO, Delta Air Lines

Organizations will assign responsibility for predictive business analytics (PBA) to various operating functions, although which line management function may be in the best position to endorse and drive the adoption of predictive business analytics is still a matter of judgment, appropriate resources, leadership, and culture. Is it marketing? Operations? Sales? Might it be the finance and accounting function? That function already has a propensity for quantitative analysis. It is in its DNA. Whichever functional group is chosen, the practices, tools, and (most important) its contributions to management decision making are still essential.

RESISTANCE TO CHANGE AND PRESUMPTIONS OF EXISTING CAPABILITIES

Some organizations may believe because they hired or trained employees with analytical skills that they have fulfilled the need to be analytical. But there are misconceptions as to what analytics is really all about. To demonstrate this, here is a true experience of one of the authors' work colleagues.

A large department store retailer accepted a brief meeting with this coworker for possible clarification about how analytics can increase profit lift from individual customers. The company's president, chief marketing officer, and head of customer analytics attended. They were somewhat impatient. This was because they were confident they already had an effective program in place since many of their customers used a loyalty card at the checkout counter.

The colleague described that with access to each customer's profile (e.g., age, address, gender) and purchase history, a real-time analytics system could substantially increase the probability that a customer will actually respond to an offer, deal, or intervention—and when. The first answer comes from data mining and the latter from forecasting, two of the many components of predictive business analytics.

After the brief presentation with only a few minutes of the scheduled meeting left, the head of customer analytics concluded that the company was already using appropriate techniques. The colleague then took a risk. The day prior to the meeting he had gone to one of the retailer's stores and purchased travel-size shampoo and toothpaste using his loyalty card. Then he repeated the identical purchase a second time. In the meeting he placed both receipts on the table, and turned them over. One receipt had a discount offer for a feminine hygiene product. The other receipt's discount was for cat food. My colleague, a male, has no pet. The chief marketing officer asked the head of customer analytics for an explanation. The answer was: "Those were among the hundred high-profit-margin products that are being promoted this month."

In this example, there was no true connection to the individual customer. And the checkout register did not have sufficient technology to access quickly in real time customer-specific deals. The three executives had a kind of an epiphany. They are now piloting a store entrance kiosk where customers can swipe their loyalty cards and receive personalized discounts and offers.

The kiosk substantially improves and increases sales compared to the checkout register method. How does the kiosk know what specific discount or deal to offer? That requires statistical analysis of different customer behaviors (e.g., Amazon.com's website message: "Others who bought what's in your shopping cart also bought X"). Early results from the retailer's pilot kiosk program were substantial. For the check-out register receipt offers a 1.8 percent response rate was the norm. The response rate rose to 30 percent for the real-time store entry kiosk.

The point here is not to proclaim that quants and statistics jockeys are swanky and smart. The intended point is that applying statistical analysis, data mining, and forecasting with a goal of optimization is now in reach—and some organizations that may think they are apply-ing these methods are only just starting to develop them.

It may be that the ultimate sustainable business strategy is to foster analytical competency of an organization's workforce. Today managers and employee teams do not need a doctorate in statistics to investigate data and gain insights and foresight. Commercial software tools are designed for the casual user. Geeks are chic, and the accounting and finance function can lead this predictive business analytics movement. However, improvement in skills and competencies will be needed. Here is why.

EVIDENCE OF DEFICIENT USE OF BUSINESS ANALYTICS IN FINANCE AND ACCOUNTING

Research[1] by CFO.com reported deficiencies in current uses of analyt-ics in finance. Roughly half of the 231 companies surveyed reported being less than "very effective" at incorporating information for stra-tegic and operational decision making purposes. Thirty-six percent of the respondents identified management intuition and experience as the primary decision criteria when making strategic and operating decisions. Only 17 percent said that statistical analysis and modeling are primary decision criteria, and 36 percent respondents reported that their companies make "little or no use" of more sophisticated techniques.

Fifty-three percent of the respondents said that robust modeling and analytics should play a greater role in their organization's deci-sion making. Finance executives appear willing to make the kind of investment needed to improve their ability to access and analyze busi-ness performance information. Seventy-six percent of the respondents anticipated that their companies will make at least a moderate invest-ment in linking operational data to financial results.

Research by the IBM Institute for Business Value[2] finds that the group of surveyed finance functions that demonstrate the highest effectiveness across the entire CFO agenda excel at two capabilities: (1) finance efficiency brought about by process and data consistency, which helps unlock the power of analytics, and (2) business insight to drive enterprise performance. Note the reference to the *power of analytics*.

The study also states that this same group consistently applied five transformation enablers throughout their journey. These are:

1. Addressing technology.
2. Enabling sequential adoption of standard processes.
3. Using new operating models.
4. Applying better analytics (again note the reference to analytics).
5. Improving workforce efficiency.

The message from these two studies is clear. Analytics is playing an increasingly important role with the CFO function. Analytics comes in many flavors, including but not limited to segmentation, correlation, regression, and probabilistic analysis.

SOBERING INDICATION OF THE ADVANCES YET NEEDED BY THE CFO FUNCTION

Another research study, this one by the Data Warehouse Institute,[3] states that "finance can be a powerful agent of organizational change. It can leverage the information that it collects to assist executives and line of business managers to optimize processes, achieve goals, avert problems, and make decisions." The study goes on to say that "forward-thinking finance departments have figured out how to transform themselves from back-office bookkeepers to business partners. They have learned to partner with the information technology (IT) department—more specifically, the business intelligence (BI) team—whose job is to manage information and deliver a single version of corporate truth. In so doing, they have liberated themselves from manual data collection and report production processes so they can engage in more value-added activities."

The research study further states that the finance function should be empowered to explore data on its own without IT assistance, and that "armed with analytical insights, the finance department can collaborate with business managers to optimize pricing, reduce inventory, streamline procurement, or improve product profitability. They can help business managers evaluate options, such as whether to add more salespeople, change commission fees, partner with a new supplier, or change merchandising assortments."

The study makes a sobering statement by saying, "Unfortunately, the majority of finance departments have yet to adopt this new role to a significant degree. Our survey shows that although the finance department has made strides toward becoming a trusted partner with the business, it still has a long way to go. Less than half of financial professionals who responded to the survey believe their finance department, to a high degree, helps the organization 'achieve its objectives' (41 percent), 'refine strategies' (35 percent), 'drive sales' (29 percent), or 'optimize processes' (29 percent). In fact, more than 20 percent of finance professionals gave their finance teams a low rating in these areas, with a larger percentage saying in effect that the finance department does little or nothing to help the business 'optimize processes' (43 percent) or 'understand and help drive sales' (50 percent)."

MOVING FROM ASPIRATIONS TO PRACTICE WITH ANALYTICS

A problem with the research studies referenced is they describe what the CFO function *could* be doing with analytics, with some blunt survey results describing the sizable gap from the *could be/should be* to the *why aren't we?*; but they do not provide tangible examples of the vision. Let's consider a few.

Customer Profitability Analysis to Take Actions

There is a trend for customers to increasingly view suppliers' products and standard service lines as commodities. As a result, what customers now seek from suppliers are special services, ideas, innovation, and thought leadership. Many suppliers have actively shifted their sales and marketing functions from being product-centric to being customer-centric, through the use of data mining and business intelligence[4] tools to understand their customers' behavior—their preferences, purchasing habits, and customer affinity groups. In some companies the accounting function has supported this shift by reporting customer profitability information (including product gross profit margins) using the activity-based cost/management (ABC/M) principles described in Chapter 10. However, is this enough?

It is progressive for the accounting function to provide marketing and sales with reliable and accurate visibility of which customers are more and less profitable. The company can also see why by observing the visibility and transparency of the internal process and activity costs that yield each customer's contribution profit margin layers. Often, sales and marketing people are surprised to discover that due to special services their largest customers in sales are not their most profitable ones, and that a larger subset of customers than believed are only marginally profitable—or worse yet, unprofitable. Exhibit 12.1 depicts a classic "whale curve" of customer profitability. But a ranking of

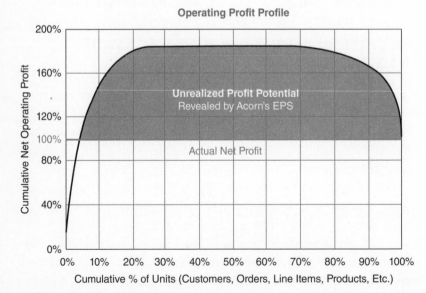

Exhibit 12.1 Operating Profit Profile

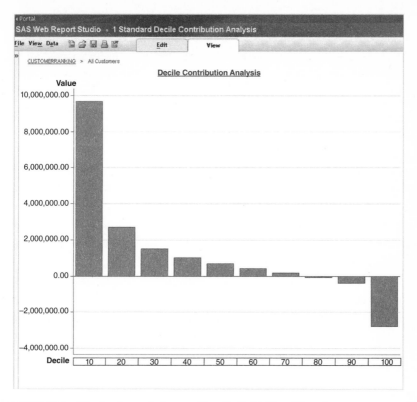

Exhibit 12.2 Why Are Some Customers More Profitable Than Others?
Source: Copyright © 2010 SAS Institute Inc. All rights reserved.

profit—from highest to lowest—of each customer does not provide all the information as to why. This ranking is illustrated in Exhibit 12.2. It is a start but without giving all the answers. This is where data mining and analytical techniques can answer the "why?" and "so what?" questions.

The use of ABC data leads to activity-based management (ABM). There are some low-hanging-fruit insights from ABC data. For example, one can see relative magnitudes of activity costs consumed among customers. There is also visibility into the quantity of activity drivers—such as the number of deliveries—that cause activity costs to be high or low. But this does not provide sufficient insight to differentiate highly profitable customers from lower-profit or unprofitable customers.

One can speculate what the differentiating characteristics or traits might be, such as a customer's sales magnitude or location. But hypothesizing (although an important analytics practice) can be time consuming. It is like finding a diamond in a coal mine. One cannot flog the data until it confesses with the truth. In attempting to identify the differentiating traits between more and less profitable customers, the major traits may not be intuitively obvious to an analyst. A more progressive technique is to use data mining and advanced statistical analytics techniques. This involves the use of segmentation analysis based on techniques involving decision trees and recursive partitioning. These techniques can give the sales and marketing functions insights into what actions, deals, services, offers, unbundled pricing, and other decisions can elicit profit lift from customers.

The goal is to accelerate the identification of the differentiating drivers so that actions or interventions can be made to achieve that high-payback profit lift from varying types of customers. Analysts using ABC/M have benefited from applying online analytical processing (OLAP) multidimensional cubes to slice and dice data. Even greater benefits and better decisions can come from applying data mining and predictive business analytics.

Rationalizing and Validating Key Performance Indicators in a Strategy Map and Balanced Scorecard

How do executives expect to realize their strategic objectives if they look at only financial results like product profit margins; return on equity; earnings before interest, taxes, depreciation, and amortization (EBITDA); cash flow; and other financial metrics? These are really not goals—they are results. They are consequences. As previously mentioned, measurements are not just about *monitoring* the summary dials of a performance scorecard. They are about *moving* the dials of the operational dashboards that actually move the strategic scorecard dials.

Worse yet, when measures are displayed in isolation from each other rather than with a chain of cause-and-effect linkages, then one cannot analyze how much influencing measures affect influenced measures.

This is more than just leading indicators and lagging indicators (see Chapter 5). Those are timing relationships. A performance scorecard reports the causal linkages and key performance indicators (KPIs), often with the clarity that comes from a well-thought-through strategy map. Any strategic measurement system that fails to start without first defining linked and aligned KPIs to its strategy and operational targets and/or reports measures in isolation is like a kite without a string. There is no steering or controlling, and eventually it will be lost in the clouds.

A strategy map's companion scorecard, on its surface, serves more as a feedback mechanism to allow everyone in the organization, from frontline workers up to the executive team, to answer the question: "How are we doing on what is important?" More important, the scorecard should facilitate analysis to also know the why, the how come, and the what are we doing about it.

To go one step further, a truly complete performance scorecard framework should have predictive business analytics embedded in it (see MetLife's journey in Chapter 6). An obvious example would be correlation analysis to evaluate which influencing measures have what degree of explanatory contribution to influenced measures. Imagine a balanced scorecard's strategy map where the thickness of the KPI arrow reflects the degree of explanatory contribution. That is how analytics embedded in a methodology brings more value. With strategic KPI and operational performance indicator (PI) correlation analysis, scorecards and dashboards become like a laboratory to truly optimize size and complexity. And consider that the thicker arrows (i.e., higher correlation) could mean to provide greater budget funding since those levers appear to drive higher results of other KPIs.

Moving from Possibilities to Probabilities with Analytics

What could possibly affect an organization's performance results? At the operational level, sales order volume could be up or down. Prices of purchased commodity materials like steel or coffee could be up or down. On a strategic macroeconomic level, consumer demand could be up or down. From a risk management perspective, weather fluctuations could adversely affect the best-laid plans.

How could you know the impact, including the financial impact, as these ranges of possibilities occur at various levels? There are three broad ways: (1) a single best guess; (2) the worst, baseline, and best likely outcomes; and (3) a probabilistic scenario of the full range of outcomes. They all include predictions with analytics.

1. **Single best guess.** Most organizations plan for results based on their managers' best assumptions of what they estimate. For example, in the annual budgeting exercise, managers forecast sales mix volume, labor rates, and prices of purchases. Each is a single-point estimate, and the accountants aggregate them to produce a single budget.

2. **Worst, baseline, and best likely outcomes.** The more advanced organizations consider three ranges of outcomes: worst, baseline, and best likely outcomes. Separate predictions are made for the key variables in the plan. Then the three overall possibilities are calculated. This provides a sense of the range of outcomes. These organizations might individually test the sensitivity of the key variables by increasing or decreasing them one at a time to see the effect and outcome.

3. **Multiple probabilistic scenarios.** The most advanced organizations take this process to its ultimate limit: from three scenarios to the full range of possibilities. That is, they estimate the probability distribution of each variable, perhaps as percentage increments from the base (e.g., −20 percent, −10 percent, 0 percent base, +10 percent, +20 percent). By combining these, they move from the three single-point outcomes to viewing a distribution curve of dozens and conceivably hundreds or thousands of outcomes. The benefit is they can have more certainty about the increasingly uncertain world they operate in. In addition, the variables become understood as drivers of the results where the level of each one may be able to be proactively managed in advance of its occurrence. These three levels are illustrated in Exhibit 12.3.

The breadth and granularity of the distribution curve increase as the probability ranges for each variable are segmented, as more variables (not just the key ones) are added, and as each variable is subdivided (e.g., from a product family to its individual products). The

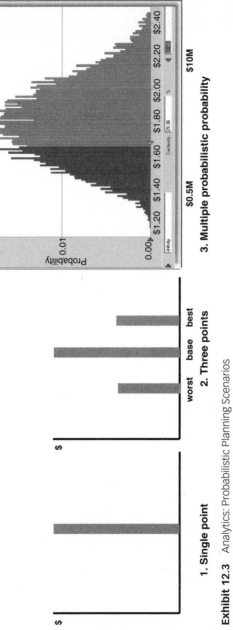

Exhibit 12.3 Analytics: Probabilistic Planning Scenarios

three-scenario approach gives a limited view of risk in contrast to the multiple probabilistic distribution curves. With the latter, sensitivity analysis can become very refined, including automated increases and decreases of each variable to determine which variable drivers are having more impact.

Now take this process to an even higher level by increasing the time interval frequency of reforecasting one or more (or even all) of the variable drivers.

What influences the accuracy and quality of the distribution curve? A critical influence is the forecasting of each variable. If the baseline is way off, then moving it up or down by increments is also going to include error.

APPROACHING NIRVANA

To achieve this best practices approach requires a combination of predictive business analytics capabilities, reliable forecasting techniques (e.g., Monte Carlo methods), and a powerful computational software engine. If this is supplemented with robust reporting, visualization, and analytical power, then it is nirvana. The full range of probabilistic outcomes can be viewed and at more frequent time intervals approaching near real time. The benefits are endless. Risk management becomes scientific. Rolling financial forecasts replace static and fixed-in-time annual budgets. Drivers can be proactively managed, such as supply chain logistics and inventory management.

Predictive business analytics is becoming a hot term with enterprise performance management. With this opportunity to move from just discussing the possibilities to understanding the factors impacting an organization and also taking actions based on the interdependent probabilities, is anyone surprised? The organization shifts from possibility to probability—managed probability—of outcomes.

CFO FUNCTION NEEDS TO PUSH THE ENVELOPE

Research by Ventana Research[5] has confirmed that the gap between current and potential use of analytics remains wide. It reports that information technology should be a particular focus because most finance organizations are not using IT assets as intelligently as they could. In particular, the finance function often focuses only on efficiency and neglects opportunities to use IT to enhance its effectiveness. Finance functions have made considerable progress in addressing their basic information needs (referred to as twentieth-century reporting requirements), but most are a long way from providing the more complete, next level of information that can be used to improve performance (their twenty-first-century requirements).

The benchmark research of this study shows there is important information that employees could receive—or already do receive—that would improve their organization's performance and help align its actions to strategy. Information deficits combined with poorly designed processes can severely limit how well all departments, including the finance function, do their jobs. The study's recommendations are that CFOs and senior finance department executives focus on these three areas:

1. Push the envelope when it comes to management reporting. To improve performance, companies must link more operational and financial data, make information available sooner, and provide a richer set of data, including leading indicators for the business unit and relevant information about competitors, suppliers, and factors that drive demand for the company's products or services.

2. Have a disciplined, sustained process in place to address information technology barriers, especially infrastructure complexity, and to enhance the use of enterprise resource planning (ERP) systems. Typically these are the root causes of issues preventing finance organizations from improving process execution and preventing the disconnections that obstruct better alignment of strategy and execution.

3. Assess where there are shortfalls in the people, process, information, and technology dimensions of key financial functions; then define a plan with specific objectives and timetables that addresses these shortfalls.

Pursuing the application of analytics is common sense. One could argue that this study omitted as a root cause barrier the natural resistance to change and preference for the status quo. Without analytics, insights and understanding for better decision making are limited.

A CXO'S LETTER TO FUTURE EMPLOYEES: EMBRACE ANALYTICS

The following letter, while hypothetical, serves as a challenge to future executives, managers, and staff to craft their careers using their inherent capabilities rather than relying too heavily on technology and current trends.

Dear young new employees,

You have an opportunity to change the world; but I am worried about you. Understandably, you are probably not interested in a finger-wagging lecture from an old fuddy-duddy and grandfather like me. But that is not my intent, so please hear me out. I am the CXO of the organization you work for, so I suggest you consider what I am about to communicate to you.

Here's my main concern: It's possible that you are overly obsessed with social media. There is more to life than Facebook, video games, YouTube, Internet surfing, and endless texting. Sure, each past generation has had its share of new gadgets and technologies to become immersed in—but none compare to what's available to this generation.

Don't get me wrong; the Internet and smartphones are great. But they can also be time-consuming distractions that keep you from focusing on more important things—like career-building and learning activities that prepare you for the future.

By no means am I proposing that you abandon social media and the endless wave of new technologies. Instead, I have a suggestion that allows you to make the most of your technological savvy and social media skills while planning for a future career: Gain proficiency and competency with applying analytics. Now is a great time to focus on a career using analytics to support decision making. The application of analytics to gain insights and foresight and solve problems is an emerging trend in all fields—with endless possibilities.

For example, you probably already enjoy examining statistics in sports or survey polls. Those examples just scratch the surface, as there are thousands of other uses of analytics waiting for you to wrap your brains around. An example of applying analytics in the business world you will soon enter is identifying the types of customers to offer the best deals to, like many suppliers do. And analytics can be applied in fields of medicine, insurance, supply chain logistics, energy management, and crime prevention, to name just a few. I'll say more about analytics shortly. But first, I'd like to discuss the importance of focusing on the activities that will best prepare you for the future.

Perils of Constantly Being Online

Researchers claim that the development of the adolescent brain can be altered due to constantly switching tasks—and consequently be less able to maintain focus and set priorities. Is this a good thing? Both focus and priority setting are highly important for future career success. My fear is your brain is being improperly wired.

You might argue that adults have contributed to my concern by providing schools with computers, Internet access, and software. It is true that educators desire to teach you in the same digital environment you are being raised in, which in many ways is a good thing. But when I read about how many hours you spend texting, browsing Facebook, or playing video games, it concerns me. A *New York Times* article described a 14-year-old who sent and received 27,000 texts in a month! I realize that not everyone participates in such extreme behavior, but at some level an uncontrolled use of digital devices can addict you to a virtual world—not the reality that you will be living in as an employee of an organization. Computers and the digital world are not just for entertainment but also for learning.

I also realize that your distraction with technology is rivaled by your acquired skills by applying technology. Many of you are discovering how to grow your interests, like making videos, which can be invaluable in your work careers. However, a balance is needed. I want you to develop critically needed competencies and identify what type of work you may like, but I don't want your grades to suffer; and there is evidence of this. Yes, being technologically savvy will give you an edge over those who are not. But there is a limit. Consider what MIT professor Sherry Turkle explains in her book, *Alone Together: Why We Expect More from Technology and Less from Each Other*.[6] She observes that people are increasingly functioning without face-to-face contact, and as a result young people's identities are being adversely shaped.

Starting with the Basics

No doubt your generation is far ahead of mine when it comes to knowing how to use the latest technologies. But does that knowledge come at the expense of experiencing the most basic, traditional forms of learning that are so valuable? How often have you read a book or watched a meaningful movie without special effects?

I am thankful that during my childhood and early adult years I spent quality time with friends, developing social skills without having to think about checking for voice or text messages. My friends and I made up games, learning how to negotiate through problems when something happened that was not in the rules we'd made up. It's amazing what valuable life lessons—and learning opportunities—can come from such simple activities.

Embrace Technology and Social Media—and Use Them to Your Advantage

Again, just because I am imploring you to start with the basics does not mean that I'm suggesting you should abandon new technologies. Innovation will (and should) continue forever. In fact, I propose the opposite—embrace information technologies and their power to solve problems. Analytics plays a key role in such problem solving. We now live in an exciting period in history. I personally feel so lucky to have been schooled with foundational concepts during the latter half of the twentieth century and now enjoy exploiting them with twenty-first-century technology.

And please do not misinterpret me that social media are not important. I actually feel just the opposite. The application of social media is accelerating in business and commerce. It provides a way for people across the world to easily communicate and offers fast, efficient, and effective ways to learn. It allows organizations to converse with customers in unimaginable ways. And social media and analytics go hand in hand. For example, data mining tools are becoming more powerful at sweeping through mountains of unstructured text data to detect positive and negative sentiment (which can be gathered from social media sites) about one's company or competitors in nearly real time.

Business-oriented social media sites, like LinkedIn, can be very valuable for building a network of professional contacts. Such sites are a great way to use social media for two very beneficial purposes: to learn and to influence. So there are many useful ways for you to communicate with Facebook and texting—but in moderation. And if you do choose to embrace analytics, you'll have the skills to build and defend your thoughts and ideas with fact-based support.

Focusing on Analytics Now Will Enhance Your Career

You will be thankful if you invest more personal time and energy now in becoming more analytical. Intuition, gut feel, posturing, and office politics are commonly determining factors when making decisions. However, they often lead to the wrong decisions. Organizations are increasingly relying on fact-based information—derived from analytics. Therefore, it takes smart, technologically savvy people with analytical skill sets to deliver the information needed for sound decision making. And your generation has just the characteristics needed to successfully fill that need.

Analytics is used in almost every field imaginable—health care, insurance, supply chain logistics, energy management, law enforcement, and more—so job opportunities are plentiful.

So now you have some good reasons for channeling your social media and technological skills in ways that will benefit your career. However, I am not your mother or father telling you what to do. If you are like those in any young generation that preceded you, it is natural to be somewhat rebellious—and I was, too. But please consider your future and reflect on my advice. If you devote more time being focused on learning, especially about analytics, you will ultimately have a more satisfying career—and maybe even make the world a better place while you're at it.

Sincerely,

Your CXO

SUMMARY

What we have learned in this chapter is that predictive business analytics can be embedded into the various enterprise performance management (EPM) frameworks. Most EPM frameworks and systems are excellent at answering the what and why about processes. An example in the CFO's accounting and finance function is measuring and reporting the profit margin layers of each customer that in total equate to the company's aggregate income statement. However, additional questions needing answers are *so what?*, *who cares?*, and *then what?*. Where should we focus and what decisions and actions do we take? And what will be the impact of them if taken? That is where predictive business analytics becomes a valued contributor to superior performance.

We learn that organizations can apply predictive business analytics to assist planning by moving beyond exploring the possibilities to the probabilities.

A key point is that achieving results from business analytics does not come easily. Leadership must provide vision and inspiration. The chapter concludes with an emphatic plea from a CXO to employees to embrace analytics as not only a way to enhance an employee's career and improve the organization's performance but also to address challenges of the global society.

NOTES

1. "Gearing Up for Growth: Financial Analytic Capabilities for Changing Times," CFO Research Services, May 2011, available at www.cfo.com/whitepapers/index.cfm/displaywhitepaper/14574582?f=search

2. "Journey to a Value Integrator," IBM Institute for Business Value, 2010, available at www-935.ibm.com/services/us/gbs/thoughtleadership/ibv-journey-to-new-value-integrator.html.

3. "Transforming Finance: How CFOs Use Business Intelligence to Turn Finance from Record Keepers to Strategic Advisors," Data Warehouse Institute, First Quarter 2010.

4. Data mining is the process of extracting patterns from large amounts of stored data by combining methods from statistics and database management systems. It is seen as an increasingly important tool to transform unprecedented quantities of digital data into meaningful information, nicknamed business intelligence, to give organizations an informational advantage. It is used in a wide range of profiling practices, such as marketing, surveillance, fraud detection, and scientific discovery.

5. "Financial Performance Management in the 21st Century—A CFO's Agenda for Using IT to Align Strategy and Execution," Ventana Research, 2007.

6. Sherry Turkle, *Alone Together: Why We Expect More from Technology and Less from Each Other* (New York: Basic Books, 2012).

CHAPTER **13**

Organizational Challenges

Everybody has accepted by now that change is unavoidable. But that still implies that change is like death and taxes—it should be postponed as long as possible and no change would be vastly preferable. But in a period of upheaval, such as the one we are living in, change is the norm.

—Peter Drucker, *Management Challenges for the 21st Century* (1999)

On the shelves in the business topics section of any bookstore are numerous books about leadership and management. Many hail the importance of executives' rallying the workforce with inspiration. In our careers most of us have seen examples of leadership that reflect their individual desire for power more than a duty to improving organizational performance. This book is about equipping managers and employee teams to help their organization be better, faster, cheaper, and smarter.

Muscle or brain? Strength or smarts? Shouldn't we choose the latter in both cases? Why?

The primary source for improvements in organizational effectiveness and decision making is shifting toward the use of analytics of all flavors. Traditional approaches like 1980s management by objectives (MBO), bullying employees, and hollow wall banners of rhetoric

("Quality Comes First") are being superseded by deploying and integrating business analytics.

Applying predictive business analytics from the CEO's top desk to each employees' desktop, tablet, smartphone, or whatever mobile device coming next enables an organization to solve complex business problems, manage performance to achieve measurable objectives with targets, drive sustainable growth through innovation, and anticipate and manage change. Just having a functional capability for predictive business analytics is important, too (see Chapter 4). In Ann All's blog "Process Management Is Weak Link in Real-Time Data Chain,"[1] she describes this well. She observes that "companies are having and will continue to have problems with all of the data they are collecting. It takes time and effort to run reports and get them to the relevant people and additional time for those people to tell the relevant systems what to do, assuming the right systems are in place."

Applying predictive business analytics results in making proactive, forward-looking decisions that go beyond low-end query-and-reporting questions like "What happened?" "How many?" and "How often?" to answer high-impact questions like "Why did it happen?" "What will happen next?" and "What is the best that can happen?"

Most analysts would prefer to have an organization with *Star Trek*'s Spock-like logic and analytical skills than one like Rocky Balboa punching meat carcasses in a freezer.

THE OBSTACLE COURSE FOR GETTING BUY-IN

A Personal Perspective from Gary Cokins

Careers sometimes have more to do with luck and circumstances than being smart and competent. However, a key for a successful career is to have luck to meet opportunity by being prepared.

Be passionate. Passion along with curiosity drives discovery. Passion is the mysterious force behind nearly every step-change in a process or introduction of a new idea.

If you always tell the truth, then you do not have to remember what you said. I have a true confession to make—I have two loves. These involve my relationship with problem-solving analytics and improvement methodologies. So what is my love problem?

The Quest to Get Buy-In for Ideas

Until about three years ago, my main interest was explaining the "how-to" for applying analytics. I have implemented analytical techniques. I'm a practitioner. I am often told I have a gift to explain complex things in a way that a common person can understand them. I love explaining to people how things work and inspiring a vision of how those same things can work much better in the future. Well, for this section of this chapter, I might fail in giving an easily understandable explanation that you can grasp. Love is very complex! But let me give it a try.

What happened to me three years ago was I was smitten. A competing suitor of my "how-to" love appeared. It is my new "why-to" love—explaining the benefits of *why to* apply analytics. They both compete for my attention. What happened was that as I concluded my seminars or discussions with potential users of analytics, I began asking this question: "Since analytics is so logical, proven, and beneficial, why is its adoption rate by organizations so gradual and slow?" Eureka! A flood of reactions gushed from people, describing many diverse barriers and obstacles. I found myself personally and increasingly attracted to these "why-not" and "why-to" discussions in contrast to my "how-to" lectures. When I witness examples of applying analytics, it takes my breath away. However, discussions about "why-not" and "why-to" are now capturing my heart. My dilemma of two loves is a nice problem to have. I love what I do.

Organizations seem hesitant to adopt analytics. Is it evaluation paralysis or brain freeze? Most organizations make the mistake of believing that applying analytics is 90 percent math and 10 percent organizational change management with employee behavior alteration. In reality it is the other way around—it is more likely 5 percent math and 95 percent about people.

WHAT IS THE PRIMARY BARRIER SLOWING THE ADOPTION RATE OF ANALYTICS?

With hindsight, we now realize that past barriers impeding the adoption rate are easily removable. That is, *technical barriers* such as disparate data sources or so-called dirty data now have software solutions like extract, transform, and load (ETL). Problems like insufficient data are also surmountable with a little effort. We also now realize that *analytical modeling design deficiency barriers,* such as weak models for evaluating customers for their future sales potential, can be knocked down with experienced consultants, better training courses, or reading earlier chapters of this book. Other barriers are misperceptions that analytical techniques are too complex or initial failures with prior pilot projects. But these are not showstoppers, and they too can be overcome.

What type of barrier continues to primarily obstruct the adoption rate of analytics? That barrier category is *social, behavioral, and cultural*. These obstacles include people's natural resistance to change, fear of knowing the truth (or of someone else knowing it), reluctance to share data or information, and "we don't do that here." Never underestimate the magnitude of resistance to change. It is natural for people to love the status quo.

An example of this social and arguably political barrier is a conflict between the information technology (IT) function and analysts—a proverbial brick wall. There will need to be a shift from face-to-face adversarial confrontation to a side-by-side collaborative relationship to remove this wall. Part of the problem is how IT and analysts view each other.

Analysts view IT as an obstructionist and uncooperative gatekeeper of data without the skills to convert that data into useful information. Experienced analysts want easy and flexible access to the data and the ability to manipulate it. They want a set of capabilities for investigation and discovery. Analysts view IT as staff who manage a set of technologies and whose main goal is to "keep the lights on and the trains running on time."

In contrast, IT increasingly views users as competitors who want to solve problems but not have to operate the solutions (i.e., systems)—they just make it harder to better manage capacity costs by using too many IT resources. And IT sees users as a risky group that has low regard for data governance and security.

Analysts need speed and agility to be reactive and proactive, which requires them to be closer to the data for analysis and better decision making. Both IT and its users will need to collaborate and compromise by better understanding and appreciating each other's changing roles.

A BLISSFUL ROMANCE WITH ANALYTICS

My heart pounds faster when I hear or read about analytics. I have learned that ambiguity and uncertainty should be an analyst's friend. Why? If getting answers were easy, an analyst's salary would probably be lower!

However, a problem with removing behavioral barriers to deploy analytics is that almost none of us have training or experience as organizational change management specialists. We are not sociologists or psychologists. However, we are learning to become like them. Our adoration for the "why-to" and its motivating effects on organizations should be driving us as an obsession. The challenge is how to alter people's attitudes.

One way to remove cultural barriers is to acknowledge a problem that all organizations suffer from their imbalance for how much emphasis they should place on being *smart* rather than being *healthy*. Most organizations overemphasize trying to be smart by hiring MBAs and management consultants with a quest to achieve a run-it-by-the-numbers management style. These types of organizations miss the relevance of how important is to also be healthy—assuring that employee morale is high and employee turnover is low. To be healthy, they also need to ensure that managers and employees are deeply involved in understanding the leadership team's strategic intent and direction setting. Healthy behavior improves the likelihood of employee buy-in and commitment. Analytics is much more than numbers, dials, pulleys, and levers. People matter—a lot.

When organizations embark upon applying or expanding their use of analytics, they need two plans: (1) an implementation plan and (2) a communication plan. The second plan is arguably much more important than the first. There are always advocates for a new project, but there are also naysayers. Knowing in advance who the naysayers are is critical to either win them over or avoid them (see Chapter 4 for some hints at getting started).

WHY DOES SHAKEN CONFIDENCE REINFORCE ONE'S ADVOCACY?

Here is some disturbing research[2] from the field of psychology that relates to the social barrier. It deals with why people actually hang on to their ideas more strongly even after they learn their ideas have been proven wrong. Using tests with a control group, the researchers revealed that the more that people doubt their own beliefs, then paradoxically the more they are inclined to support and lobby for them.

The test subjects who were confronted with evidence that challenged and disproved their beliefs subsequently advocated them even more aggressively compared to the control group.

This finding is bothersome because applying fact-based quantitative statistics and logical methodologies is far superior than making decisions based on intuition and gut feel. How can we transform someone who is a "Dr. No" into a "Dr. Know"? Shouldn't executives and managers desire to gain insights or know something about the future before their organization gets there? How valuable should it be to them to know things that their competitors do not know?

EARLY ADOPTERS AND LAGGARDS

Another barrier involves organizations that are too distracted with problems and prefer to search for quick fixes. The urgent crowds out the important. These organizations do not take the time to solve problems with a better way. In our personal lives, many of us have no problem making everyday decisions, such as whether to purchase a smartphone or join a social network. How can we as individuals make decisions so quickly, while organizations often struggle and are slow to react?

The field of marketing scientifically examines influences on the rate of adoption of products, services, and technology. Everett Rogers, a business researcher, developed his Diffusion of Innovations model with five categories of adoption: (1) innovators, (2) early adopters, (3) early majority, (4) late majority, and (5) laggards. Which category best describes many organizations with respect to adopting analytical methods?

Innovators and early adopters quickly move forward because either they are having financial difficulties needing new solutions or they are very progressive and driven to continuously seek a competitive edge. In contrast, the late majority and laggard organizations either are risk averse with resistance to change or lack visionary leadership.

However, there is another possible explanation for the laggards— they are too distracted. There is no doubt that increasing volatility is part of the problem. The world seems to be operating in an increasing speed-up mode with increasing unpredictability and accelerating change. Is it possible this is a false read, and big fluctuating swings and unexpected events just appear that way because of 24-hour news coverage collected from all corners of the earth? Are there really more earthquakes and floods? Or do global media simply report more quickly and immediately than in prior decades?

Examples of volatility include changes in consumer preferences, foreign currency exchange rates, and commodity prices. New trends contributing to volatility can develop quickly, such as oil dependence and the emergence of country economies (e.g., India and Brazil). Un-anticipated shocks can come from occurrences like the Asian tsunami, H1N1 virus outbreak, global economy crisis, euro currency shocks, and recently, the civil unrest in North African Arab countries. The Internet, global communications, social networks, and relaxation of international trade barriers have introduced vibrations and turbulence compared to relatively smooth rises and falls of the past decades.

But is increased worldwide volatility a good enough reason not to adopt or at least test predictive business analytical methods? Analytics can be adopted by late majority and laggard organizations, regardless of volatility with proven methods and techniques, such as with pilot projects and rapid prototyping for a proof of concept.

When executive teams are distracted with firefighting, reacting to surprises, or internal politics, then the urgent squeezes out the important. Business and government face a vastly different environment than they did a few short decades ago. The Internet had just begun to be a transformational force, the Cold War was on, China was just emerging as a major economic player, and European countries had their own currencies. During that time, the global environment wasn't as much of a factor in their decision making. Today, organizations operate as though perpetual crises are the new normal, so multiple distractions, while trying to react, are a given.

But such distractions aren't an excuse for always being reactive instead of proactive. Being focused on solving problems does not mean that an organization cannot pursue opportunities to improve how it manages and improves its performance.

Organizations that want to move beyond the laggards category must take on the mentality of the early adopters, who understand the importance of using predictive business analytics to enhance decision making and align employee behavior and priorities to execute the executive team's strategy. They must be proactive, not just reactive. Most important, remember that it's never too late to go from being in the middle of the pack to taking a commanding lead over your competitors.

The popular Harvard Business School professor Michael Porter defined three accepted, generic strategies for a company: cost leadership, differentiation, and focus.[3] However, they are all vulnerable today because competitors can more quickly take actions such as reduce costs, imitate a company, or invade a company's market niche. An organization's best defense against the competition is the ability to quickly make intelligent decisions—which can easily be accomplished by implementing analytics. Organizations that achieve competency with analytics would be able to sustain a long-term competitive advantage.

HOW CAN ONE OVERCOME RESISTANCE TO CHANGE?

Resistance to change is arguably the root cause of the slow adoption rate problem. A proven approach to accelerating the acceptance and learning rate is to create an analytics competency function as described in Chapters 4 and 5.

We have relied on a simple formula as a guide for how to overcome resistance to change. It is $(D \times V \times F) > R$, where R stands for resistance. Do not underestimate how large R is; it can be enormous. Therefore, in the equation if D, V, or F is zero or small, then their multiplicative combination will not exceed R. You will need all three factors in great abundance in order to overcome R. Okay. So what are the D, V, and F?

■ D is *dissatisfaction with the current state*. Unless people have discomfort, they will not be interested in changing anything. It is a proverbial burning platform or sense of urgency.

■ V is a *vision of what a better state looks like*. When people see a different view of their circumstances that can lead to an improved condition, they will consider changing.

■ F is often neglected—it stands for *first practical steps*. Large amounts of D and V are not enough to overcome a large R. If people think the vision (V) is overly theoretical, complicated, costly, or impractical, they will not pursue changes to realize that vision. You need F to make the vision attainable. Examples of F are early success stories based on pilot projects and rapid prototyping with iterative remodeling techniques to demonstrate value and prove concepts. These accelerate learning and get more buy-in.

Most enthusiastic and well-meaning managers try to promote their vision—the V in the formula. They get excited about analytics. Our advice from experience is to first focus on the D and not the V. Here is why.

Change will result only when people feel compelled to change. For example, at your annual health physical, your doctor suggests losing a few extra pounds so that you will not have high blood pressure. On your way home, you are ready to have your usual late afternoon snack of doughnuts and coffee. Remembering the doctor's caution, you stop but have only the coffee and skip the doughnuts. You have just experienced behavioral change.

Having high levels of dissatisfaction and discomfort, the D, is your best lever to influencing colleagues and getting buy-in. But dissatisfaction is often latent and not overt. You will need to create the required discomfort in your colleagues and managers. This can be achieved by using the Socratic method of asking colleagues questions, such as: "How do we know which types of customers to retain, to grow, to acquire as new, or to win back, and how much should we optimally spend on each customer type for maximum profit lift? How accurate are our forecasts of demand?" Ask them similar questions for which you know predictive business analytics will provide informative and impactful answers with high payback.

In many cases your colleagues and executives will not have good answers. When they do not, ask them: "Is that is a good thing? How long can we want to perpetuate making decisions without knowing these answers?" If you ask these thought-provoking and deliberately disturbing questions in the right way, you will not need to spend much time on promoting your vision (V) of the equation—why to use predictive business analytics. By converting and exposing latent problems into ones evident to your executives and colleagues, you make the solutions become more obvious, understandable, and implementable.

Always remember that in the absence of facts, anybody's opinion is a good one. And usually the biggest opinion wins—which is likely to be that of your boss or your boss's boss. So to the degree your executives are making decisions on intuition, gut feel, flawed and misleading information, or politics, then your organization is at risk. Does your organization know, or do its leaders think they know? By creating doubt, one can overcome resistance to change.

Until an organization gains mastery over validly answering questions with predictive business analytics, it will plod along and muddle through improving its performance rather than accelerate value creation.

THE TIME TO CREATE A CULTURE FOR ANALYTICS IS NOW

The old organizational model for decision making is broken. The jig is up. Making decisions relying on gut feeling, intuition, office politics, past experience, and bias is giving way to using fact-based information and predictive business analytics. These allow for investigation, insights, foresight, and improvements.

Some readers may already be reacting to these observations and saying to themselves, "I've heard this exaggerated story before." Skepticism is a healthy virtue. Skepticism involves waiting for enough evidence before accepting or believing.

For many of us, belief in the value of analytics began at an early age. Math came easily to us in grade school. We enjoyed solving story problems. We liked to measure things, including time and distance.

It may be a big stretch to conclude that current organizational models that are not fully embracing predictive business analytics are broken. What is needed is a culture for analytics and accountability. The lesson is to help people measure what matters: to provide a context for what constitutes improvement, whether it is time, quality, service level, customer satisfaction, revenue, or cost.

Then, similar to watching a plant grow from the soil, watch nature grow individual skills.

Executives can formulate textbook strategies like offering highly differentiated products and services or being the lowest-cost supplier. But today these are vulnerable strategies because competitors can quickly match them. The best sustainable competitive edge will come from creating a culture for analytics and accountability—from training employees to have competencies with predictive business analytics that lead to fact-based and better, faster, and more insightful decisions.

PREDICTIVE BUSINESS ANALYTICS: NONSENSE OR PRUDENCE?

Analytics is a means to an end where the end game is performance improvement. That is, analytics is an enabler, not necessarily the root cause for improvement. And there are obviously multiple other contributors to organizational improvement, including having enough money to spend on improving and having good executive leadership.

A valid question is this: How much does the presence of employee competency with predictive business analytics impact the *rate* of organizational improvement? A little? A lot? Or somewhere in between? How do organizations improve? One answer involves the increasing attention to the topic of leadership. For example, ex-CEOs like General Electric's Jack Welch get paid large fees for speaking engagements on leadership. Does this mean that better executive leadership equates to a faster rate of organizational improvement?

It sounds logical that it does. Why? Executive leadership is mainly about two items: (1) setting strategic direction with vision, and (2) inspiring and motivating workers and partners to go there. As executive leaders get better, they observe, listen, and learn. This then results in a robust rate of organizational improvement.

As the authors of this book, our opinion on this logic is it is nonsense—part fiction and part myth. In our opinion, concentrating and centralizing decision making and power at the top have become ineffective. Yes, executives need to formulate winning strategies, but today the name of the game is implementing and executing the strategy, not just defining it.

TWO TYPES OF EMPLOYEES

There are probably dozens of ways to categorize and segment an organization's employees into types. Here is a simple but provocative segmentation of types: (1) watchers and (2) analyzers. To be sure, any employee does both. The distinction is in the weightings of how much they do of each.

Executive leaders are mainly *watchers*. They cook up ideas and projects intended to implement their strategy. Then they monitor performance against expected targets. However, too often their organization's traditional heritage and past successes blind executives from seeing insights for change. Motorola's decline is an example. Executives with power can justify the status quo by invoking dubious rationales. (Did you know that between the years 1998 and 2007, 460 of the S&P 500 companies had one or more fiscal losses?)

Analyzers, the other type of worker, are increasing in number relative to the watchers. This type of employee may not be equipped with powerful analytical software tools; but that does not prevent them from being inquisitive and investigating data to convert it into revealing information from which to gain insights and foresight.

INEQUALITY OF DECISION RIGHTS

A problem, actually an obstacle, is that analyzers have not been granted sufficient decision rights to act on their conclusions derived from their fact-based explorations. Decision rights remain hoarded at the top of the organization. Executives are in the saddle. Empowering employees with decision rights and analytical tools to attain them is the key to organizational improvement.

There is an iron law of economics that the better the decisions, then the better will be the results—and hence continuous organizational improvement will follow, financial or otherwise. It is now time for organizations to connect these dots.

Studies have shown that the two major barriers to effective strategy execution are (1) not distributing decision rights downward into the layers of the organization chart, and (2) poor cross-functional information flows.[4] Contrary to common beliefs, removing these two barriers trumps reshaping the boxes and lines in the organization chart and incentive systems.

Politicians of all nations are wrestling with how best to improve their countries' education systems. They know that in this twenty-first century the more educated and skilled their citizens are, then the higher will be their nation's economic prosperity. The same goes with an organization's employees. Organizations need a culture of being analytical.

WHAT FACTORS CONTRIBUTE TO ORGANIZATIONAL IMPROVEMENT?

So, we return to the question of how much predictive business analytics contributes to organizational improvement—relative to other factors. Our unscientific answer based on anecdotal observations is that competency with analytics is number one. Is it prudence or nonsense to embrace analytics? It is definitely wise and prudent.

Every day organizations make thousands of decisions at all levels, some big and some minor. But they all add up, and the more that decision rights are granted down into the workforce skilled with analytical competency, then the faster will be the rate of organizational improvement.

ANALYTICS: THE SKEPTICS VERSUS THE ENTHUSIASTS

Resistance to change is human nature. People are comfortable with and like the status quo. The acceptance of analytics to tackle issues related to big data is going through growing pains. The transition pits skeptics, who are typically older and shaped by managing when errors were tolerated, against typically younger enthusiasts. The margin for error is thinner now, and past buffering methods to mitigate the impact from mistakes are overly expensive and fraught with penalties. How and why are the skeptics of applying analytics different from the enthusiasts? To begin to understand the answer, let's begin with a quiz.

A Quick Quiz

What is a good nine- or ten-letter description of the emerging interest in predictive business analytics and big data that ends in *-al*?

A choice that may come to mind for many is *hysterical*. This choice reflects frenzied excitement about opportunities for business analytics to solve problems often resulting from big data. Advocates—actually enthusiasts—of analytics have become energized by the growing interest in the fields of business intelligence and data mining. But perhaps a less obvious choice of *skeptical* is an equally valid answer. Doubters and naysayers of business analytics believe that the interest in these topics is overblown and misguided.

Where Are the Skeptics Coming From?

Let us start with the view of the skeptics of analytics. Who are they? What is their profile? What is their objection to embracing and deploying analytics?

This may be an exaggeration, but here is one take on the skeptics of analytics. When they took a statistics course in college, many of them probably just wanted to pass and get the course behind them.

When the skeptics' careers were shaped, they did not have PlayStations, Nintendos, or Xboxes—no video games at all. They did not have 150 channels on cable, satellite TV, video movies, or DVDs. They had no surround sound, no smartphones, no personal computers, and no Internet.

During the skeptics' early careers, they observed and participated in company firefighting. This was actually fun for them. It kept them busy. The assertive skeptics were continuously promoted to higher job positions because of their quick wit and intuition. These types of managers are mostly not self-serving sycophants and political players (although some are). They are hard workers.

The older skeptics grew up watching television series like *Ozzie and Harriet* and *Leave It to Beaver*. At their offices—since most skeptics have been white-collar workers most of their careers—their coworkers and supervisors weren't much different from Ozzie Nelson and Ward Cleaver, the fathers in those TV series. Ozzie and Ward shaped the skeptics' values and attitudes of what the daily workday would be like. After a pleasant breakfast at home with the family, one headed to the office to shuffle papers, attend meetings, and return missed phone calls (from handwritten secretary notes).

The career experiences of skeptics did not involve punctuated change and volatility as occurs in today's sped-up world. However, it was not easy for them. Their organizations weren't static and frozen in

YBP Library Services

MAISEL, LAWRENCE, 1946-

PREDICTIVE BUSINESS ANALYTICS: FORWARD-LOOKING
CAPABILITIES TO IMPROVE BUSINESS PERFORMANCE.
Cloth   252 P.
HOBOKEN: JOHN WILEY, 2014
SER: WILEY AND SAS BUSINESS SERIES.

GUIDEBOOK.

LCCN 2013-23509
  ISBN 1118175565   **Library PO#** FIRM ORDERS

		List	49.95	USD
8395 NATIONAL UNIVERSITY LIBRAR	**Disc**	14.0%		
App. Date 2/12/14 SOBM 8214-08	**Net**	42.96	USD	

SUBJ: 1. BUSINESS PLANNING--STAT. METH.
2. BUSINESS INTELLIGENCE.

CLASS HD30.23   DEWEY# 658.4013   LEVEL PROF

YBP Library Services

MAISEL, LAWRENCE, 1946-

PREDICTIVE BUSINESS ANALYTICS: FORWARD-LOOKING
CAPABILITIES TO IMPROVE BUSINESS PERFORMANCE.
Cloth   252 P.
HOBOKEN: JOHN WILEY, 2014
SER: WILEY AND SAS BUSINESS SERIES.

GUIDEBOOK.

LCCN 2013-23509
  ISBN 1118175565   **Library PO#** FIRM ORDERS

		List	49.95	USD
8395 NATIONAL UNIVERSITY LIBRAR	**Disc**	14.0%		
App. Date 2/12/14 SOBM 8214-08	**Net**	42.96	USD	

SUBJ: 1. BUSINESS PLANNING--STAT. METH.
2. BUSINESS INTELLIGENCE.

CLASS HD30.23   DEWEY# 658.4013   LEVEL PROF

time. Occasional new products and services were developed, and new types of customers pursued. Some companies merged, divested, and acquired other companies. So there were periods of transition following those events before the skeptics' workweeks settled down to a normal pace. But just like after a passing storm, they eventually returned to shuffling papers, writing memos, and attending meetings.

Skeptics were not free from solving problems or evaluating opportunities. Those are eternal tasks in anyone's workday. What was different about the solutions developed when skeptics' careers were shaped was that the solutions just weren't that elegant—they were like Swanson TV dinners, oven-baked in aluminum trays.

Skeptics' Reliance on Buffers to Protect against Errors

Here is an example of problem solving in manufacturing that the skeptics experienced. If a supplier's shipment of component parts was going to be late, that was okay. The assembling manufacturer simply rescheduled its customers' orders, and its shipment would likely be late to the distributor or retail store. If this resulted in an out-of-stock shortage when customers wanted or needed the finished product, then their customers just dealt with it and made do. The reasoning was that sometimes it rains, and you don't have an umbrella. And Murphy's Law of the unexpected periodically sneaks up on you.

When skeptics' careers were shaped, there were no crystal balls to predict the future. But they did not need them. In manufacturing, a forecast was somehow produced every month or so, and it was used to establish plans for determining what inputs and how much to buy (e.g., raw materials, component parts) and what types of resources to hire or purchase.

When skeptics' careers were shaped, they survived using buffers to protect them from errors and missed delivery schedules. Buffers were the magic elixir that kept problems from becoming larger or more painful. There were three types of buffers that skeptics relied on related to time, flow, and resources. They would start things earlier to buffer expected finish dates, build and stock extra inventory to buffer material shortages, and add more people and equipment to buffer capacity.

Let us fast-forward to today. Skeptics recognize that the world has changed. It is much more volatile. But they still challenge the need to embrace deep or advanced analytics. When their careers were shaped, they observed people measuring something with a micrometer, marking it with a piece of chalk, and cutting it with a swinging ax. They behaved this way, too. Why be precise? Few organizations recognized the penalties and extra buffer-related expenses and investments that mitigated against imprecision and errors. Inefficiencies, long delivery lead times, and temporary shortages were tolerated by both suppliers and their customers.

Where Are the Enthusiasts for Analytics Coming From?

Let us look next at the opposite view—that of the analytical enthusiasts whose careers have been more recently shaped. Who are they? What is their profile? What is their enthusiasm (sometimes hysterically so) for embracing and deploying analytics?

Again, this will probably be an exaggeration to make the point, but here is a take on the enthusiasts. They are likely to be under the age of 50. When they took their university statistics courses, they had hand calculators and laptop computers. Some readers who graduated from college prior to 1970 may have had only slide rules.

During enthusiasts' careers, firefighting has not been an occasional need—it has been ongoing and never-ending. And its intensity is not just because there are more problems (although there are). It is because there are more opportunities requiring a sense of urgency.

These younger enthusiasts grew up watching MTV, *Friends,* and *Seinfeld*. Their sense of humor is more wry and cynical compared to that of the skeptics. Their curiosity about how things work is probably comparable to the skeptics' when they were the same age. However, the difference is that the enthusiasts have much greater ability to investigate and analyze—and with more computing power and more functional software.

In the movie *Moneyball*, Brad Pitt plays the role of the Oakland Athletics baseball team general manager Billy Beane. Just before Pitt fires the team's head baseball scout, he says (paraphrasing), "Okay. My turn. When you visit the home of an aspiring young baseball player and you tell his parents that he has a good chance of being a major league player, you don't know. You don't know." He repeats that to make his point.

This also applies to organizations, especially where skeptics dominate. Skeptics may think they know, but do they *really* know?

Enthusiasts Use Analytics to Replace Buffers

Let us revisit the example of manufacturing and distribution companies. As previously discussed, in the past the skeptics solved operational problems with buffers. But enthusiasts' careers today have been shaped by buffers that must be paper thin. Buffers that the skeptics enjoyed to protect them from the impact of problems are too costly today. These costs and penalties include surplus inventory, excessively long production and delivery lead times, extra equipment capacity, poor customer service levels, and more employees than are needed.

Analytics is reducing the size of and replacing the protective crutch of buffers. Today the enthusiasts for analytics are imaginative and visionary. Their thinking does not stop with enterprise resource planning (ERP) systems, which can schedule part production and purchasing based on forecast product demand volume, supplier delivery rates, and assembly lead times. Enthusiasts are far more imaginative than that—plus they have the analytics and computing power to be creative.

What enthusiasts do is think forwardly with probabilistic what-if scenario analysis. They do not view product distribution in a supply chain as a linear tree, branch, and leaf structure that sequences parts like elephants' trunks to tails in a circus all the way from production to the customer. Enthusiasts see opportunities in an integrated network of parts and products that exist or can be made anywhere. And they then perform iterative trade-off analysis of the interrelated variables in real time.

Enthusiasts know there are four interrelated variables that have complex interrelationships: customer service levels, lead times, demand volumes, and unit costs. Since suppliers have measured and calibrated all of the processing times and consumption rates from recent past-period data, they then know the relationships among all four variables. The analytics enthusiasts' vision is one where they start with a baseline case scenario projected into the future. (Most are already using advanced demand forecasting techniques.) They then perform what-if analysis. They change one of the variables—probabilistically—as the *independent* variable, and calculate the impact on the other three *dependent* variables. And then they change another variable—and so on.

This gives enthusiasts power to answer many questions, such as: "What is the additional inventory carrying cost if we want to improve service levels from 97 to 99 percent for our strategic customers?" These capabilities are no longer a dream or vision. They exist today.

Enthusiasts Can Win Buy-In from the Skeptics

Admittedly, these profiles of skeptics versus enthusiasts were exaggerated. They are not polar opposites but rather people residing along a continuum. But this does not remove the challenge of creating a culture for analytics.

An effective way to drive change, overcome resistance, and gain buy-in is through examples. Enthusiasts can be role models. Lead by example. Demonstrate what can be done, and it will be done.

MAXIMIZING PREDICTIVE BUSINESS ANALYTICS: TOP-DOWN OR BOTTOM-UP LEADERSHIP?

The expanding managerial movement to adopt predictive business analytics is being spurred by the needs for improved organizational performance and a sharpened competitive edge. Now that the benefits of applying analytics for insights and foresights for better decisions are being accepted, the next question is: How should an organization get the maximum yield and benefits from predictive business analytics?

Carlson's Law: Bottom-Up versus Top-Down Ideas

A trend with applying analytics is a demonstration of Carlson's Law, posited by Curtis Carlson, the CEO of SRI International in Silicon Valley.[5] It states: "In a world where so many people now have access to education and cheap tools of innovation, innovation that happens from the bottom up tends to be chaotic but smart. Innovation that happens from the top down tends to be orderly but dumb." As a result, says Carlson, the sweet spot for innovation today is "moving down," closer to the people, not up, because all the people together are smarter than anyone alone, and all the people now have the tools to invent and collaborate. An excellent example of this is how medical research and development are being conducted today by leading scientists who are forming research teams of diverse skills and competencies and are achieving break-through discoveries and cures.

A generally accepted way to drive the adoption of analytics is with executive team sponsorship and formally establishing a *competency center* for predictive business analytics. Unfortunately, the conditions are not always right for these. Executives are often distracted with firefighting or office politics. And creating a competency center requires foresight and willpower from executives, which can be a limiting factor.

We are a believers in Carlson's Law because we have observed it in the adoption of enterprise performance management methodologies. These methodologies include strategy maps, balanced scorecards, customer profitability analysis, risk management, and driver-based rolling financial budgets and forecasts. Passionate middle-manager champions more often drive change involving analytics than do executives. Why? Middle managers ask themselves, "How long do we want to perpetuate gaining understanding and making decisions the way we do now—with little or no analytical insight or hypothesis testing?"

ANALYSTS PURSUE PERCEIVED UNACHIEVABLE ACCOMPLISHMENTS

Leadership does not exist only at the top of the organizational chart. Leadership can be present in individuals below the C-suite positions. How can this be? It is because a key dimension of leadership is the art of getting a group of people to accomplish something that each individual could not do alone. Leadership does not require formal authority and command-and-control behavior.

A simple model of leadership has three components:

1. **Care.** Followers believe that a leader cares about them and the organization.
2. **Trust and hope.** Followers believe that supporting a leader will improve things.
3. **Mission.** Followers want leaders to answer the question "Where do we want to go?" so that they can help answer "How will we get there?"

Executive leaders must communicate the third component; however, middle-manager champions can exhibit the first two.

ANALYSTS CAN BE LEADERS

Experienced analysts realize that applying analytics is not like searching for a diamond in a coal mine or flogging data until it confesses the truth. Instead they first speculate that two or more things are related, or that some underlying behavior is driving a pattern to be seen in various data. They apply business analytics more to confirm a hypothesis than to randomly explore. This requires easy and flexible access to data, the ability to manipulate the data, and software to support the process. This is a form of leadership.

Leaders require moral, not physical, courage. An example of physical courage is rescuing someone from a fire. That is noble but not leadership. Moral courage is almost the opposite of a rescue. It is doing something not immediately highly valued and potentially perceived as sticking your nose in others' business. But ultimately it is seen as a helpful contribution to organizational performance improvement.

There are hundreds of examples of applying predictive business analytics. One is to identify the most attractive types of customers to retain, grow, win back, or acquire. Others involve risk management, warranty claim analysis, credit scoring, demand forecasting, clinical drug trials, insurance claims analysis, distribution route optimization, fraud detection, and retail markdown and assortment planning. The list is endless.

The investigation and discovery of what will align an organization's actions with the executive team's strategy for execution will not come from a CEO with a bullhorn or a whip. Better insights and foresight and their resulting decisions will come from analytical competency. Analysts can demonstrate leadership with the passion and desire to solve problems and discern answers—the power to know.

SUMMARY

This chapter has put a human face on broad topic of predictive business analytics. What we have learned is that the information technology for analytics is no longer the impediment for applying analytics. The obstacle is now social, cultural, and behavioral. This means that to accelerate the rate of adoption of predictive business analytics, change management must be emphasized to remove barriers.

One of prominent barriers is natural resistance to change. People prefer the status quo. A key point made with the $D \times V \times F > R$ formula is that of the three factors in the formula (i.e., dissatisfaction with the current state, vision of what a better state looks like, and first practical steps), the first one—dissatisfaction—is critical. If there is not sufficient dissatisfaction, for right or wrong reasons, then analysts should proactively but subtly create it, ideally by asking provocative questions that lead to people having doubts.

We have learned in this chapter that having the right type of leadership mind-set and desire to foster a culture for analytics can accelerate gaining competency with predictive business analytics.

NOTES

1. "Process Management Is Weak Link in Real-Time Data Chain," IT Business Edge, www.itbusinessedge.com/cm/blogs/all/process-management-is-weak-link-in-real-time-data-chain/?cs=35853.
2. David Gal and Derek Rucker, Northwestern University's Kellogg School of Management, "When in Doubt, Shout," *Psychological Research*, November 2010.
3. Michael E. Porter, *Competitive Strategy: Techniques for Analyzing Industries and Competitors* (New York: Free Press, 1980).
4. Gary L. Nelson, Karla L. Martin, and Elizabeth Powers, "The Secrets to Successful Strategy Execution," *Harvard Business Review*, June 2006.
5. "Advice for China," the *New York Times*, www.nytimes.com/2011/06/05/opinion/05friedman.html?_r=1.

About the Authors

Gary Cokins is the founder of Analytics-Based Performance Management LLC, an advisory firm located in Cary, North Carolina. He is an internationally recognized expert, speaker, and author in advanced cost management and performance improvement systems. Following receipt of an industrial engineering and operations research degree with Tau Beta Pi honors from Cornell University in 1971 and an MBA from Northwestern University's Kellogg Graduate School of Management, Gary began his career with FMC Corporation with roles in strategic planning at headquarters, controller, and operations manager. He served 15 years as a consultant with Deloitte Consulting, KPMG Peat Marwick, and Electronic Data Systems (EDS, now part of Hewlett-Packard), where he headed EDS's Global Cost Management Consulting Services. From 1997 until recently Gary was in business development with SAS, a leading provider of enterprise performance management and business analytics and intelligence software.

In 1988 with KPMG, Gary was trained by Robert S. Kaplan and Dr. Robin Cooper of the Harvard Business School on implementing activity-based cost/management (ABC/M) systems.

Gary was the lead author of the acclaimed *An ABC Manager's Primer* sponsored by the Institute of Management Accountants (IMA). His next six books were:

- *Activity Based Cost Management: Making It Work*
- *Activity Based Cost Management: An Executive's Guide*
- *Activity Based Cost Management in Government*
- *Performance Management: Finding the Missing Pieces to Close the Intelligence Gap*

- *Performance Management: Integrating Strategy Execution, Methodologies, Risk, and Analytics*
- *Strategic Business Management: From Planning to Performance*

Gary serves on advisory boards for the International Monetary Fund, www.kpilibrary.com, www.smartdatacollective.com, http://bigfatfinanceblog.com/, www.information-management.com, www.iianalytics.com, and www.informs.org.

He is Certified in Production and Inventory Management (CPIM) by the American Production and Inventory Control Society (APICS). He is a speaker for and member of many committees of professional societies, including the Consortium of Advanced Management International (CAM-I), APICS, the Supply Chain Council, the Council for Supply Chain Management Professionals (CSCMP), the International Federation of Accountants (IFAC), the Institute for Management Accountants (IMA), the American Association of Accountants (AAA), and the American Institute of CPAs (AICPA).

He can be reached at garyfarms@aol.com or gcokins@garycokins.com.

Lawrence S. Maisel is President of DecisionVu Group, Inc., a management consultancy specializing in corporate performance management, financial management, and IT value management. He is a seasoned business executive who has successfully demonstrated abilities to provide leadership in strategy and financial management and in information technology with numerous experiences in financial services, insurance, communications and media, and pharmaceuticals industries. He has developed business strategies, managed and improved business performance, implemented business systems, and designed solutions to increase operating performance and shareholder value.

He has assisted numerous clients and senior-level executives in designing and implementing in-depth performance management systems, including balanced scorecards for corporate and operating business units, as well as designing and improving processes and systems for business reporting and analysis and for planning, budgeting, and forecasting.

He has extensive industry experience with global organizations, including MetLife, TIAA-CREF, Citigroup, JPMorgan Chase, the Federal

Reserve System, American International Group (AIG), General Electric, XL Capital, Boeing, Honeywell, Ford, Bristol-Myers Squibb, Pfizer, Merck, News Corporation/Fox Entertainment, and many other Global 1000 industrial and financial services companies.

Larry has held senior executive positions at PeopleSoft, at Balanced Scorecard Collaborative, and as Executive Partner in Charge of KPMG Consulting's Strategy and Financial Management Consulting practice. He has also held management positions, including CEO and CFO.

Larry cocreated with Drs. Kaplan and Norton the balanced scorecard approach, coauthored with Drs. Kaplan and Cooper *Implementing Activity-Based Cost Management: Moving from Analysis to Action*, authored *Performance Measurement: The Balanced Scorecard Approach*, was former Editor in Chief of Warren Gorham & Lamont's Corporate Finance Network and *Journal of Cost Management*, and a member of the editorial advisory board of the *Journal of Strategic Performance Measures*. Recently, he authored IFAC's International Good Practice Guidance (IGPG) on "Predictive Business Analytics."

He was an adjunct professor at Columbia University's Graduate Business School, where he taught courses on strategy and performance management, and was a guest lecturer at Northwestern University's J.L. Kellogg Graduate School of Management. He has also developed and delivered numerous training programs for private, public, and professional organizations.

He has spoken at numerous business and user conferences on a variety of topics and is one of the foremost leaders in the areas of corporate performance management and predictive business analytics.

He was a member of Forrester Research's Senior Advisory Board and of Cognos's Innovation Center Advisory Board, is a contributing author for *Business Finance* magazine, and has served on numerous advisory boards for both private and public organizations, often as chairman or lead adviser.

Larry is a CPA and holds a BA in economics from New York University and an MBA in corporate financial management from Pace University.

He can be contacted at LMaisel@DecisionVu.com.

Index